WRITERS AND THEIR WORK

ISOBEL ARMSTRONG
General Editor

ROBERT BURNS

From an original illustration of Robert Burns by Colin Hunter McQueen
reproduced by kind permission of the artist.

ROBERT BURNS

Gerard Carruthers

NORTHCOTE

BRITISH
COUNCIL

First published in 2006 by Northcote House Publishers Ltd, Horndon, Tavistock, Devon, PL19 9NQ, United Kingdom.
Tel: +44 (0) 1822 810066 Fax: +44 (0) 1822 810034.

British Library Cataloguing-in-Publication Data
A catalogue record for this book is available from the British Library

ISBN 0-7463-1172-9 hardcover
ISBN 0-7463-1177-X paperback

Typeset by PDQ Typesetting, Newcastle-under-Lyme
Printed and bound in the United Kingdom

Contents

Acknowledgements		vi
Biographical Outline		vii
Abbreviations and References		xii
1	Reading Burns	1
2	Burns the Bard	7
3	Religion	25
4	Politics	43
5	Women, Love and the Body	62
6	Folk Culture	80
7	Song	95
Notes		109
Select Bibliography and Discography		111
Index		115

Acknowledgements

My knowledge of Robert Burns has been much enhanced over the years by dialogues of one kind or another with Alexander Broadie, Ted Cowan, Sarah Dunnigan, Richard Finlay, F. W. Freeman, David Hewitt, R. D. S. Jack, Thomas Keith, Colin Kidd, the late Donald Low, Alison Lumsden, Kirsteen McCue, Liam McIlvanney, Andrew Noble, Donny O'Rourke, Thomas R. Preston, Alan Rawes, G. Ross, Lucie and W. W. Roy, Patrick Scott, Peter Westwood, Christopher Whatley and Hamish Whyte. It is a particular pleasure to acknowledge encouragement during the writing of what follows from two of the finest Burns scholars, Kenneth Simpson and Norman Paton. I am greatly indebted to Colin Hunter MacQueen, who generously provided the inside illustration of Burns, to Irvine Burns Club, and particularly to the assistance of John Inglis, for kindly granting permission to reproduce J. E. Christie's painting 'The Vision', and to the support of Douglas Gifford, Alan Riach and Rhona Brown in the Department of Scottish Literature at the University of Glasgow.

This is a book that discusses Burns's often cross-grained cultural identity. I dedicate it to Our Holy Redeemer Primary and St Andrew's High schools, Clydebank, places where I was first taught that human identity is a complex and precious thing not to be taken for granted.

Biographical Outline

1759   Robert Burns is born on 25 January at Alloway, Ayrshire, the eldest child of William Burnes or Burness and Agnes Broun, where his father is a seven-acre tenant.

1760   Burns's brother, Gilbert, born on 28 September. Five other siblings, three girls and two boys, born (1762–71).

1765   Robert and Gilbert briefly attend a school at Alloway Mill run by William Campbell; they are then taught by 18-year-old John Murdoch, a private tutor hired by William Burnes and four neighbours until 1768.

1766   William Burnes takes a twelve-year lease on a seventy acre (Scots) farm at Mount Oliphant, two miles from Alloway, for an annual rent of £45.

1767   On Murdoch's departure, William personally educates Robert and Gilbert, procuring for the purpose expensive books on geography, theology and letters by accomplished stylists.

1772   During the summer Robert and Gilbert go week about, while the other attends to work at Mount Oliphant, to Dalrymple School (here improved penmanship is the main focus of their education).

1774   Inspired by Nellie Kilpatrick, his companion in the autumn harvest, Burns composes his first work, the song 'O Once I Lov'd'.

1775   Attends Hugh Rodger's school, Kirkoswald, to study mathematics and surveying.

1777   William Burnes takes lease of the 130 acre Lochlea farm, Tarbolton, at the high annual rent of £1 an acre.

1778–9   During the winter Robert attends dancing classes at Tarbolton, much to his father's displeasure. At some point around this time, William becomes unable to pay the rent at Lochlea. In the resulting dispute with the landlord, an Ayr merchant, David McLure, William was left financially ruined, even though eventually the harsh terms of the lease were legally adjudicated to have been irregular.

1780   With himself as president, Burns forms, with Gilbert and five friends, the Tarbolton Bachelors' Club, a debating society of the type fashionable in the age of Enlightenment.

1781   On 4 July Burns is inducted as a Freemason in St James's Lodge, Tarbolton. During that summer he is apprenticed as a flax dresser at Irvine, on the Ayrshire coast.

1782   On 1 January the flax dressing shop in Irvine burns down and Robert returns to Lochlea.

1783   In January, Burns wins £3 prize money for his flax seed. In April he begins his first *Commonplace Book*, in which until 1785 he records 'Observations, Hints, Songs, Scraps of Poetry &c.' In May, William Burnes's failure to pay his rent results in the issuing of a writ of sequestration. This represents a stage prior to full bankruptcy, where an inventory of possessions to be poinded is made. William appeals against the writ. In the autumn Robert and Gilbert sublease the 118 acre farm at Mossgiel, near Mauchline, from Gavin Hamilton for £90 per annum, as a refuge for their family in the expectation of William's bankruptcy.

1784   On 27 January William wins an appeal at the Court of Session averting his bankruptcy. He dies on 13 February and the family move from Lochlea to Mossgiel, a farm that experiences poor crops for the next four years. It is probably some time between November of this year and the spring of 1785 that Burns first meets Jean Armour.

1785   Burns's first child, Elizabeth, to Elizabeth Paton, a servant at Lochlea, is born on 22 May. In June he writes his first poem in Scots, 'The Death and Dying Words of Poor Mailie', having already written a handful of poems in English and some songs in Scots (a total of around two dozen previous items).

1786   In the early months of this year Burns books a berth on the ship *Nancy*, bound for Savannah-la-Mar (Jamaica), set to sail in the summer. In March, James Armour, father of

Jean, opposing the betrothal of his daughter to the poet, has a lawyer cut out the names of the couple in a document they had written agreeing to their marriage. At some point shortly afterwards, with Jean seemingly now compliant with her father's stance, Burns courts Margaret Campbell ('Highland Mary'). On 3 April, he signs the name 'Burnes' for the last time in a letter, thereafter adopting 'Burns' as his surname. On 14 May Margaret Campbell goes to Greenock to see her friends and relatives, possibly arranging her affairs so that she can join Burns on his voyage to Jamaica. On 22 July, Burns transfers his share in Mossgiel to his brother Gilbert. During July and August, Burns and Jean are rebuked in church on three consecutive Sundays for committing fornication. On 31 July *Poems Chiefly in the Scottish Dialect* is published at Kilmarnock. During September, Burns repeatedly 'postpones' his voyage to Jamaica. On 3 September, Jean gives birth to twins. At some point, probably in October, Burns receives news that Margaret Campbell has died of a fever at Greenock. Burns begins his correspondence with Mrs Frances Anna Dunlop on 15 November. He arrives in Edinburgh on 29 November to plan a new edition of his poems. On 9 December, Henry Mackenzie reviews his poems in *The Lounger* and coins for the poet the epithet of the 'heaven-taught ploughman'.

1787   On 17 April the 'Edinburgh edition' of *Poems Chiefly in the Scottish Dialect* is published, subscribed to by over 1300 individuals. On 23 April, Burns sells the copyright of the book to William Creech for 100 guineas. From 5 May until 1 June, Burns tours the borders with his friend the lawyer Robert Ainslie. This is the first of the tours that Burns projected 'to make leisurely pilgrimages through Caledonia; to sit on the fields of her battles; to wander on the romantic banks of her rivers; and to muse'. The first volume of James Johnston's *Scots Musical Museum* appears on 22 May, including three songs by Burns. In late June, Burns undertakes a tour of the West High-lands. In mid-August, Burns complies with a writ that had been served for paternity of her child by the Edinburgh servant May? (Meg) Cameron. From 25

August until 16 September, Burns tours the Highlands with William Nicol, and in October he tours Stirlingshire with Dr Adair, a relative of Mrs Dunlop, where, in Clackmannan, he is 'knighted' by Mrs Catherine Bruce, a Jacobite claiming descent from Robert the Bruce, king of Scotland. In late October Burns becomes resident in Edinburgh, where he begins to work hard on contributions for the *Scots Musical Museum*. On 4 December in the capital he meets Agnes (Nancy) McLehose, 'Clarinda', a middle-class lady estranged from her husband: their correspondence begins on 28 December. Some time during late 1787 or early 1788 Burns begins an affair with the servant-girl Jenny Clow, who gives birth to his son (probably in December 1788).

1788   Burns requests the patronage of Robert Graham of Fintry to allow him to pursue a career in the crown excise service. On 14 February the second volume of the *Scots Musical Museum* is published, with thirty-two songs by Burns. On 3 March, Jean bears Burns short-lived twins, and in April the poet at last acknowledges her as his wife. On 18 March he signs the lease for a farm in Ellisland, Dumfriesshire, at which he settles on 11 June. From April to May, Burns receives training in the excise service at Mauchline, in which he is commissioned on 14 July. In December, Jean joins Burns in Dumfriesshire.

1789   Burns is enthusiastic about the outbreak of the French Revolution. His favourite son, Francis Wallace, is born on 18 August. On 1 September he begins work as an excise officer for a salary of £50 per annum.

1790   During the winter Burns suffers from a lingering illness and is depressed about the prospects of the farm at Ellisland. On 27 January he is listed as eligible for the promoted post of supervisor in the excise. In February the third volume of the *Scots Musical Museum* contains forty songs by Burns. On 24 July, Robert's 13-year-old brother, William, dies. On 1 November, Burns completes 'Tam o' Shanter'.

1791   Burns's daughter Elizabeth is born on 31 March to Helen Anne Park, who works at the Globe Inn, Dumfries. On 9 April, Jean gives birth to a son, William Nicol. On 10 September, Burns gives up Ellisland and becomes a full-time employee in the excise. During October, probably, Burns moves to a house in the centre of Dumfries with Jean and four children. In Edinburgh in December he takes his leave of Agnes McLehose, who sails to Jamaica to join her husband in January 1792.

1792   Burns is appointed as an exciseman to the Dumfries Port division in February, which brings him £20 a year additional salary. In August the fourth volume of the *Scots Musical Museum* is published, containing forty-seven songs by Burns, and a number of other items which he had collected (bringing his total contribution to sixty songs). On 16 September, Burns agrees to contribute to George Thomson's *Select Collection*. On 21 November a daughter, Elizabeth Riddell, is born to Jean.

1793   In February, William Creech publishes in Edinburgh an expanded two-volume edition of *Poems Chiefly in the Scottish Dialect*, to the annoyance of Burns when his complimentary copies are delayed. In May the first volume of Thomson's *Select Collection*, with seven songs by Burns, is published. On 19 May, Burns moves his family to a larger house in Mill Vennel, Dumfries. From late July until 2 August, Burns tours Galloway with John Syme.

1794   On 12 August Burns's son James Glencairn is born. During late December, Burns is appointed acting supervisor of excise at Dumfries.

1795   On 31 January Burns joins the Dumfries Volunteers, a local militia formed in response to the fear of invasion from France. In September his daughter Elizabeth Riddell dies. In December Burns is seriously ill and unable to work.

1796   On 21 July Burns dies in Dumfries either of rheumatic fever, or possibly of brucellosis. As a militiaman, he is buried with full military honours on 25 July, and a son, Maxwell, is born on the same day. In December the fifth volume of the *Scots Musical Museum* is published, with thirty-seven of Burns's songs, including 'Auld Lang Syne'.

Abbreviations and References

Quotations of Burns's poetry and prose are taken from the following editions, abbreviated in the text as shown:

L   *The Letters of Robert Burns*, edited by J. De Lancey Ferguson and G. Ross Roy, 2nd edition, 2 vols (Oxford: Clarendon, 1985). Reference is made to the volume number and then the page number.

LL   *Ae Fond Kiss: The Love Letters of Robert Burns and Clarinda*, edited by Donny O'Rourke (Edinburgh: Mercat, 2000). Reference is made to the page number.

MM   *The Merry Muses of Caledonia*, facsimile edition prepared by G. Ross Roy (Columbia, South Carolina: University of South Carolina Press for the Thomas Cooper Library, 1999). Reference is made to the page number.

PS   *The Poems and Songs of Robert Burns*, edited by James Kinsley, 3 vols (Oxford: Clarendon, 1968). Reference is made to the item number rather than the page number.

1

Reading Burns

Robert Burns performs a similarly 'bardic' function for Scotland
as William Shakespeare does for England and, like Shakespeare,
Burns is a writer whose part in the expression of a seemingly
univocal 'national identity' sits somewhat at odds with his own
trammelled cultural location. Where Shakespeare may have
been a secret Catholic, spiritually at odds with a state establish-
ment that increasingly adopted his imaginative vision of English
history, Burns successfully marshalled contradictions in his own
and in Scotland's identity. A Lowland poet of Presbyterian
background, Burns inhabited the eighteenth-century tradition
of poetry in Scots that, in its original Episcopalian, Catholic,
aristocratic, Tory and Jacobite leanings, was largely hostile to his
cradle culture. As with Shakespeare, arguably smuggling the
Catholic purgatory into *Hamlet*, so too with Burns, who made his
native Ayrshire oblivious to the fact that the 'Habbie Simson'
stanza (later renamed the 'Burns' stanza in popular conception)
and the 'Christ's Kirk' stanza, which he had imbibed from the
Scots poetry revival of the east coast of Scotland, were not part
of, and, indeed, traditionally sat ideologically at odds with, the
dominant traditionally puritanical Presbyterian culture of Scot-
land. Burns, like Shakespeare, is a great cultural transformer,
transplanting many 'alien' ideas into his 'native' soil.

As well as bringing to bear on Ayrshire the predilections of the
Scots poetry revival of the eighteenth century (which included
also, for instance, the depiction of enjoying food and drink as a
means of cocking a snook at what it took to be the puritanical
tendencies of Calvinist Presbyterianism in Scotland), Burns also
played a large part in the Lowland acceptance of Highland
culture. Though in jocular mode, William Dunbar, poet of the
fifteenth century, had written that there was no music in hell

1

except for the bagpipes, and this expressed an essential hostility towards the Highlands in Lowland Scottish culture more or less intact down to Burns's time. Burns's collection and recreation of Jacobite song and his extension of human sympathy to high-landers across his *oeuvre* helped begin to shift the racial hatred and fear of the highlander, which had reached its height in the alarm caused by the rebellion of 1745.

If Burns was a synthesizer of disparate strands of Scottish culture, the same can be said for Burns the 'British' poet. As much influenced in his imaginative landscape by the English poets John Milton, Alexander Pope and William Shenstone (to name but a few) as by the Scots language writers Allan Ramsay and Robert Fergusson (to say nothing of the influence of 'problematic' Anglo-Scots such as James Thomson), Burns is a very catholic British eighteenth-century writer, who has as primary colours on his poetic palette Augustan didacticism and the emotional tumult engendered by the age of sentiment. Ideas of mutually exclusive canons of 'English' and 'Scottish' literatures are essentially inventions of the twentieth century, and the encouragement of discrete national identity following the First World War. Albeit a construction itself, in the nineteenth century Matthew Arnold had promulgated a diffuse notion of 'Celtic' literature that extended to English literature, as well as the literatures of the supposedly 'Celtic' countries of the British Isles.

By the twentieth century, however, with T. S. Eliot and F. R. Leavis (on the 'English' side) and the rise of the cultural and political nationalism that constructed 'Scottish literature' as a contemporary discipline, lines of 'English' and 'Scottish' 'tradition' came to be drawn. These were somewhat exclusive, as they over-discriminated between writers on such one-dimensional criteria as 'the language' that they used or the geographical space that they inhabited (not to mention a whole series of somehow racially transmitted 'national characteristics' that do not bear much close scrutiny). What such over-tightened 'traditions' overlooked, for instance, was that for someone of Burns's Presbyterian background, John Milton, as a dissenting Protestant writer, was more naturally a part of his intellectual and cultural background than was the case for many English people. Burns's bicultural facility in English as well as Scots, as demonstrated by his entertaining and brilliantly written letters (mostly in standard English), has often been read by Scottish critics in the terminology of 1960s psychobabble as a 'crisis of identity', and here again we see a limp inflexibility to the polyvocal, boundary-denying and cosmopolitan energies drawn upon by most writers of any stature.

The misreading of Burns as a phenomenon predates the twentieth century, and the poet himself might be seen to bear some culpability here. As we will see, Burns collaborated in the construction of own image as an untutored writer, the 'heaven-taught ploughman', when this was far from the case. That he did so was not simply a marker of the limited class space available to Burns, but was a choice to some extent predicated by the poet's immersion in the age of sentiment and sensibility that placed such a high premium on 'nature' and 'feeling'. If this had a certain (and long-term) cost in the failure by readers to grasp the literary amplitude of Burns, in another sense the poet's self-placement was a contribution to the emerging Romantic age. Burns is a harbinger of an age about to explore nature in a new way, where humanity and the natural world are seen to stand much less sharply apart than had previously been the case, and of the lyric suffusion (in both his poetry and his songs) of the Romantic period.

One of the ironies in the Burns canon is that the manicuring of Burns's 'natural' image actually occluded the presentation of some of his most daringly outspoken productions, such as 'Holy Willie's Prayer' (not published in 'official' form during his lifetime) or *The Merry Muses of Caledonia* (where some of the poet's most iconoclastic and most tender treatments of the human body are contained within a volume originally only passed around in manuscript form among Burns's Edinburgh drinking club, the Crochallan Fencibles). In what follows the term 'reserved canon' is coined for such material, as opposed to Burns's much more tightly controlled 'official canon', comprising, mainly, *Poems, Chiefly in the Scots Dialect* (the 'Kilmarnock edition' of 1786) and the two expanded 'Edinburgh editions' of the same name of 1787 and 1793. Burns's songs found their major vehicles in James Johnston's *The Scots Musical Museum* (1787–1803) and George Thomson's *Select Collection of Scotish Airs* (1792–1818), in the former of which, especially, Burns could be

3

more slyly experimental in passing off his own material as being 'traditional' (here we find another paradox where Burns sometimes fabricates tradition out of himself, in distinction to fabricating himself from 'traditional' or 'natural' materials). Burns's 'falsification' in his own creativity, then, runs quite deeply, even as it is part of a project to champion the sensibility of 'nature' in which he sincerely believed.

What is most cogent across both Burns's official and his reserved canons is his Enlightenment sensibility (again, a long-standing critical truism that will be countered in the chapters that follow is that the rationalistic Enlightenment stands in huge antipathy to poetry in Scots during the eighteenth century). From the Enlightenment in Scotland and in Europe, Burns imbibed an interest in psychology and a historical sophistication, which, when taken together, help explain his alternate iconoclasm and respect towards his own cultural background (the ability, as we shall see, one moment to lampoon Calvinist Presbyterianism in its puritanism, and the next to celebrate the dogged independence of this mindset). If one single influence marks out Burns's path-breaking impetus as a poet it is the doctrine of 'sympathy' or putting oneself in the shoes of others (often very different, disparate kinds of 'others') that he imbibed from reading his favourite philosopher, Adam Smith. Burns is in receipt of formative influences from the traditions of the Scots vernacular revival, the Enlightenment, his own Presbyterian, peasant culture (which, alongside his Enlightenment mindset, provides Burns most powerfully with his often iconoclastic view of authority), as well as of the whole tradition of British eighteenth-century poetry (mainstream pastoral predilections, Augustan didacticism and so on) and the attitudes of the age of sentiment. Burns, then, is a poet of complex formation even if, like any powerful writer, the final choices and constructions of his poetry cannot be absolutely explained but by a certain individual dash.

Burns's individuality has been a particularly fraught area in his reception in Scotland. On the one hand, Burns has been read almost as an impersonal oracle distilling the native wit and wisdom of Ayrshire and of Scotland, so that, for instance, some Burnsians have spoken traditionally of his verse epistles as though these were simply the product of robust, rural Ayrshire good sense, rather than schooled, as they were, in Burns's own voracious reading of this mode in Pope, Allan Ramsay and others. The result is that the verse epistle, which in the Augustan age was seen as an appropriate one for urbane and civilized gentlemen, is notionally transformed as representing couthy, country common sense. If Burns is himself a driver of this transformation in writing verse epistles from the perspective of a tenant farmer rather than a gentleman, and if this transformative process is justifiable license in a creative writer, the downside is that here, precisely, is a location where Burns's 'reading' (his literary rather than his 'folk' culture) comes to be underestimated.

As so often with Burns there is a series of gains and losses in his innovative inhabiting of 'personal' poetic space. For a long time this was especially apparent in the fabrication of a highly conservative Burns, used in moralistic fashion by Burns Clubs and expatriate Scots to reflect a misleading image of the Scot who was essentially pious, rural and 'simple' in outlook (in contradistinction, it can be argued, to the reality of the nineteenth-century imperial Scot in his aggressively urban and colonial tendencies). The reaction against this image of the 'kailyard' (cabbage-patch) Burns was most aggressively seen in the 1920s and 1930s, when Scottish modernist writers such as Hugh MacDiarmid and Edwin Muir saw the influence of Burns as largely harmful in Scottish literary consciousness. Muir referred to both Burns and Walter Scott as 'sham bards of a sham nation', inferring that these authors fabricated romantic, escapist versions of Scotland in their writings and all too easily lent themselves to propping up harmful myths of a cogent, virtuous nation, when the reality was that mainstream Scotland from the time of Burns and Scott was neither of these things, in being both nebulously British and enthusiastically imperialist overseas in hand with her southern partner.[1] With more levity, Muir even wittily teased Scotland's reception of Burns as a kind of inverted Christ figure, where the notorious sexual exploits of 'the bard' were enjoyed vicariously on the page by a nation of douce Presbyterians too timid to carry the burden of their own sins. In this latter formulation Muir actually reminds us that writers are not necessarily responsible for the use of their work made by others.

5

As we shall see, Burns was certainly not shy of passing critique on what he regarded to be the most pressing political, cultural and social issues of Scotland and Britain in his own day. Burns's support for the French Revolution and for the downtrodden (which increasingly from the 1920s won Burns huge admiration in Russia) should not be ignored, since his were among the most heartfelt literary statements of this kind in the 1780s and 1790s. Nonetheless, it is the case that a number of Burns's political and bawdy poems emerged only slowly and patchily into print over the course of the nineteenth century. The first editor of the collected Burns in 1800, James Currie, was intent on making money for Burns's widow and family, and sought to expurgate some of Burns's more scatological productions as being inappropriate to a polite audience. However, Currie, part of the English radical circle of William Roscoe active in the parliamentary reform and pro-abolitionist causes, was not necessarily acting out of political conservatism. Some critics have attempted to smear Currie in this way when he was proceeding merely with a caution that mirrored Burns's own with regard to his possession of a 'reserved' canon and an official 'published' canon. In recent years attempts to present an impeccably 'leftist' bard have involved inflating and ignoring the facts no less than the previously conservative incarnations of Burns, in a formation that the present writer has termed the 'New Bardolatry'.[2] As we shall see, Burns in his political expression (though broadly in favour of the revolutions, political and cultural, in his lifetime), as in his utterances with regard to those other large 'signposts' in his life and career – religion, sex, folk culture, song, and his own coinage as a bardic poet – is sometimes ambiguous and even contradictory. What might be more remarkable, however, given the fraught and cross-grained times that produced Burns and in which he lived, would be a poet who was all too glibly sure of himself and completely coherent in his utterances – potentially less remarkable in another way, though, since he would likely have been a much less creatively febrile artist.

2

Burns the Bard

The publication of *Poems, Chiefly in the Scottish Dialect* at Kilmarnock in Ayrshire on 31 July 1786 marks the official unveiling of the work of a man who was to become a cultural phenomenon in terms that are worldwide. Prior to his first book, Robert Burns had already achieved regional celebrity status during 1785 as a poet with a brace of satires ('The Holy Fair' and 'Holy Willie's Prayer') on the predominant Calvinist religion of his locality. The manuscript circulation of these and other pieces, most notably a series of verse epistles written during 1784–5, marks the poet out as part of the satellite Ayrshire Enlightenment, taking its cue from the metropolitan Scottish versions of this milieu in Edinburgh, Glasgow and Aberdeen. An independent tenant-farmer at Mossgiel in Mauchline, Ayrshire, since 1783, Burns was also from 1781 a Freemason and an intimate acquaintance of many of the professional class (including lawyers, merchants and teachers) around the county town of Ayr, and it was in such circles that Burns's poetic iconoclasm and urbanity were first enjoyed.

The publication of the 'Kilmarnock edition', as Burns's first book became known, was supported by 612 advance subscriptions, though these were concentrated, principally, on fewer than a dozen individuals (for instance, Burns's friend the lawyer Robert Aiken took out 145 of these on behalf of many other like-minded admirers whom he knew to constitute a ready-made market). The book was a venture born out of financial necessity. Burns's farm, which he worked principally with his younger brother Gilbert, was barely profitable, and he was at this time talking to friends, whether seriously or not, of leaving for the West Indies, where he would find employment as a manager among the slave plantations. It may be, however, that Burns's projected emigration represented only proud posturing, since he was a highly strung man during 1786. From March to July of that year, James Armour, father of Jean, who was eventually to become Burns's wife in 1788, strenuously attempted to prevent his daughter from having anything to do with the poet, broadcasting widely in the vicinity his view of the opprobrious nature of Burns, and going so far as to have a lawyer physically remove the names of the couple from an irregular but binding marriage contract they had made between them. The fact that Jean was pregnant did not simply predispose James to accept the match, and this astonished Burns underpinning his avowed aim to leave for Jamaica; and it may also have galvanized his determination to produce his book as a way of demonstrating a higher worth than his future father-in-law estimated for him. In this entangled period, of which biographers have yet to write an entirely cogent narrative, Burns was also involved with 'Highland Mary' (Margaret Campbell). The poet may have wanted her to accompany him to the West Indies, he may have contracted a secret marriage with her, valid within Scots law, and she may have been pregnant by him, but there is no conclusive evidence for any of these repeated staples of the received lore. What is certain is that Margaret Campbell died, probably during October 1786, and it is not clear whether this fact, or the success of the Kilmarnock edition, which by this time had begun to receive admiring reviews in the Edinburgh periodicals, caused him to divert his previous plans, if real plans they were, to go abroad.

If the detailed facts surrounding Burns's personal life at this time remain murky, the Kilmarnock edition reveals the more certain cultural pulse of Burns the poet. Among the forty-four poems in the book are to be found 'For the Author's Father' and 'The Cotter's Saturday Night', the first explicitly and the second implicitly a tribute to Burns's late father. From scant funds, William Burnes had insisted upon a good education for his eldest sons, Robert and Gilbert, periodically financing their attendance at elementary schools, and also through hiring, in effect, a private tutor (the cost and services shared by a number of other tenant-farmers like Burnes), first at the family smallholding in Alloway and then at the farm of Mount Oliphant. This young tutor, John Murdoch, provided not only foundation skills in literacy and numeracy, but also more advanced instruction in rhetoric, French and some Latin as well. Burns, who was occasionally in conflict with his father during his youth, for instance, over the poet's desire to take dancing lessons, and who dropped the 'e' from the family name as early as 1780 in his correspondence indicating a desire for a certain degree of independence in identity, was certainly conscious of a huge formative debt to his father both in terms of the gift of education and also with regard to his forgiving, far from entirely puritanical religious outlook, as attested to by the poet in the tender 'For the Author's Father'.

A rather different Scottish influence from that provided by the poet's father with his traditional Presbyterian veneration of education is to be found in 'The Death and Dying Words of Poor Mailie' (PS 24). This poem is most probably Burns's first effort in Scots (the poet having written several poems in English and around ten, mostly Scots, songs prior to this), and shows the influence of the Scots vernacular poetic tradition of the eighteenth century. The two main channels of this tradition are to be found in the work of Allan Ramsay, which Burns probably began to read in the late 1770s, and Robert Fergusson, whose poems were an electrifying discovery for Burns during 1783. 'Poor Mailie' is in the mode of comic dying words found in Ramsay's masterpiece *Lucky Spence's Last Advice* (1718), which underneath its facetious surface imparts something serious about society. Ramsay's Lucky Spence is a brothel-keeper whose practical advice to the girls she is leaving behind serves to exemplify the rampant mercantilism that Ramsay sees dominating early eighteenth-century Britain. Burns goes one better than Ramsay in ventriloquizing the last words of a ewe, but has no social critique as such to mount, except in so far as he has his protagonist recommend good agricultural practice to her master and moral propriety to the young son and daughter she is leaving behind. Mailie delivers her final wisdom to a farm labourer who is to tell the farmer that if he is to keep a larger herd of sheep they should be allowed to rove around at will, rather than being tethered as was so often the case with the small-scale animal husbandry that was the norm for most of the eighteenth century in Scotland. This simple innovation, then beginning to be felt in Scotland, would lead to healthier livestock, so farming theory of the day was currently explaining.

9

Burns shows himself not only to be a student of enlightened agricultural writing, but also attentive to the moral discourse that was a strong strand of Scottish Enlightenment thought in having Mailie recommend to her children the most decent behaviour:

An' may they never learn the gaets,   [ways
Of ither vile, wanrestfu' *Pets!*   [restless
To slink thro' slaps, an' reave an' steal,   [breaks in fences etc
At stacks o' pease, or stocks o' kail.
So may they, like their great *forbears*,
For monie a year come thro' the sheers:
So *wives* will gie them bits o' bread,
An' *bairns* greet for them when they're dead.   [weep

(ll. 35–42)

A slight piece, 'Poor Mailie' nevertheless sets out a terrain that becomes pronounced in Burns's oeuvre, that of questioning the boundary between the spheres of nature and of humanity. We have a mild satire on the presumption that nature can be made to accord with human predilections, a theme that becomes increasingly darker in Burns in keeping with the proto-Romantic reaction against 'progress' during the late eighteenth century. Related to this theme, the Scots language here begins to take on a sardonic accent in opposition to the polite, Anglified discourse associated with cultural and scientific progress among the literati of the Scottish Enlightenment.

Sixteen of the poems in the Kilmarnock edition are written in the 'standard Habbie' stanza and three in the 'Christ's Kirk' stanza. The first of these was so named by Allan Ramsay at the beginning of the eighteenth century after its use in 'The Life and Death of the Piper of Kilbarchan' (about the piper Habbie Simson) attributed to the seventeenth-century Scottish poet Robert Sempill of Beltrees. During the nineteenth century and continuing down to the present, the stanza comes to be known as the 'Burns' stanza, and this renaming is typical of the amnesia that has been engendered with regard to Burns's forbears in the eighteenth-century Scots poetic tradition. For Ramsay and Fergusson, the two stanzas were utilized as instances of what we would today call cultural nationalism. The 'Habbie' stanza has an ancient history going as far back at least as the troubadours of France, and the 'Christ's Kirk' stanza is a coinage of the medieval period, not certainly Scottish. Both stanzas become especially adopted by Ramsay in his own original poetry after the publication of 'The Life and Death of the Piper of Kilbarchan' and the poem 'Christ's Kirk on the Green' in the first volume of James Watson's *Choice Collection of Comic and Serious Scots Poems* (1706). The communal festivity celebrated in these and other poems in Watson's anthology is part of a cultural phenomenon rooted in the Stuart-loyal, 'Cavalier' culture of the seventeenth century. Watson, as a Jacobite Tory loyal to the Stuarts in exile, sees his own ideology as being at odds with the puritanical, Calvinist 'Whigs' of Scotland who had supported the 'Glorious Revolution' of 1688. The drinking songs, folk festivity and comedy of the *Choice Collection* (and most especially 'Christ's Kirk on the Green', attributed to the medieval Stuart sovereign James V) signal, then, deep political allegiance. Watson's anthology also appears at a time when the Presbyterian Whigs of Scotland are, for the most part, in favour of a parliamentary union with England that is accomplished in 1707, and Jacobites (often Episcopalians or, like Watson, Catholic) are opposed to the Union since they read this as cementing the dynastic settlement of 1689. Allan Ramsay shows his Jacobite colours in beginning to write new poetry for the eighteenth century in the stanza forms that he discovers in Watson, and in utilizing also the Scots language that, in his hands, increasingly becomes an anti-Unionist reflex. By the 1770s, when the failed Jacobite uprising of 1745–6 has put paid to any realistic chance of a return of the Stuart dynasty, Robert Fergusson, the second great poet of the eighteenth-century Scots poetry revival, displays the attitude of 'sentimental Jacobitism'. He, more than any other writer, maintains the vibrancy of the two stanzas of cultural nationalism in his work and continues to critique the puritanical 'Whiggish' outlook, as well as a mismanaged Scottish and, indeed, British polity rife with 'luxury', which Fergusson, essentially High Tory in his outlook, reads as emanating from the money-grubbing settlements of 1689 and 1707 and the consequent rise of commerce during the eighteenth century.

When the poetic 'technology', the Scots language and the stanza vehicles that Burns inherits from his two great predecessors, is considered we should realize that the Presbyterian

11

poet is in receipt of a culture not entirely 'native' to him. We begin to glimpse Burns as an artist of transformation who brings into the mainstream of 'Scottish' poetic expression elements of a politically defeated outlook. Burns, a man whose behaviour was increasingly censured by the Calvinist authorities, found the anti-Calvinist attitudes of Ramsay and Fergusson amenable, and, combined with these influences, his education in Enlightenment thought (with its emphases upon moderation in religion) also contributed to his jaundiced view of the religious background in which he had been brought up. The influence of Fergusson upon Burns was also a matter of profound emotional engagement, and single-handed Burns sought to restore the remembrance of his predecessor, who had enjoyed a reputation in Edinburgh among those of his own political complexion but who was otherwise, unlike Ramsay, not widely known in Scotland. In the Kilmarnock edition's 'To W. S*****n, Ochiltree' (PS 59) Burns, in the 'Habbie' stanza, sets up an opposition between the high society of Edinburgh in Fergusson's day and Fergusson's drudging employment as a lawyer's clerk:

O *Fergusson!* thy glorious *parts*,
Ill-suited *law*'s dry, musty arts!
My curse upon your whunstane hearts   [whin-rock – hard, dark rock
          Ye Enbrugh Gentry!
The tythe o' what ye waste at *cartes*
          Wad stow'd his pantry!   [crammed

(ll. 19–24)

This is all very well, but the implication that Fergusson died through impoverishment that could have been ameliorated by others is a dubious one. At the age of 23 Fergusson had died in the Edinburgh bedlam suffering from some difficult to specify mental disease. Burns's creation of the myth of Fergusson's damaging neglect by the Edinburgh gentry stuck, but its true significance is probably to be measured in terms of Burns's awareness of his own fragile status as a poet at this time, financially and personally beset as he was while trying to establish a career as a published poet. Nonetheless, not only was Burns using Fergusson as a potential mirror for his own melancholic circumstances, he was genuinely interested, as he

12

was in so many aspects of Scotland's historic culture of poetry and song, in reviving awareness of his predecessor, a technically excellent poet; and in 1787, when his own material success was beginning to be assured, he personally put in place the finance for the erection of a tombstone at Fergusson's unmarked grave in the Scottish capital.

Henry Mackenzie's famous pronouncement of Burns as 'this Heaven-taught ploughman, from his humble and unlettered station', made in a review of the Kilmarnock edition in *The Lounger* of 9 December 1786, is clearly ridiculous, as it underscores the mainstream cultural ignorance in Scotland of the Scots poetic revival of the eighteenth century (the ideological complexion of which was unattractive to moderate Presbyterian Enlightenment activists such as Mackenzie).[1] Mackenzie, however, was not being simply condescending, or wilfully selective, as he arrived at his estimation, but was responding to Burns's own preface in the volume. In this the poet quotes Shenstone and name-checks Ramsay and Fergusson, but makes the claim that he is a primitive, albeit in a prose of polished third person accomplishment:

Unacquainted with the necessary requisites for commencing Poet by rule, he sings the sentiments and manners, he felt and saw in himself and his rustic compeers around him, in his and their native language. Though a Rhymer from his earliest years, at least from the earliest impulses of the softer passions, it was not till very lately, that the applause, perhaps the partiality, of Friendship, wakened his vanity so far as to make him think any thing of his was worth showing; and none of the following works were ever composed with a view to the press. To amuse himself with the little creations of his own fancy, amid the toil and fatigues of a laborious life; to transcribe the various feelings, the loves, the griefs, the hopes, the fears in his own breast; to find some kind of counterpoise to the struggles of a world, always an alien scene, a task uncouth to the poetical mind; these were his motives for courting the Muses, and in these he found Poetry to be its own reward.[2]

Mackenzie and others went along with Burns's obviously contradictory construction of himself as a 'nameless Bard', as the poet defines himself in his preface, presumably because an opportunity was being presented by Burns for Scotland to add to its canon of primitivist literary output. From the 'Ossianic' productions of James Macpherson in the 1760s, Scotland had prided itself in its 'natural' ability in the creative literary imagination. Rousseau's theory of the 'noble savage' found enthusiastic reception in the Scottish Enlightenment, not only because its predominant 'moral sense' philosophy privileged the idea of untutored human capacities, but because this presented a solution to the problem that Scotland (in Anglocentric cultural presumption) was a backward, uncultured location. If the more meagre economic circumstances of Scotland and also its literary history, so trammelled and interrupted by internecine confessional and ideological dispute, were awkward facts difficult to deny in the face of England's more ample, settled, 'civilized' culture, then the idea of spontaneously arising or 'rootless' expressive genius was an attractive proposition to Enlightenment men of letters such as Mackenzie. Burns in his preface can be seen collaborating with this project even as, at the same time, he acknowledges his literary heritage in the Scots poetry tradition, to say nothing of his obvious debt to elegant English Augustan writing.

Burns's adoption of the mantle of 'bard' played to the faux-Celticism that came into vogue in the eighteenth-century, attested to in the literary taste of the Scottish Enlightenment for 'Ossian' (a legendary bard whose work Macpherson ostensibly 'recovered', though in actual fact he 'massaged' this, adding to and massively amplifying fragmentary original material translated from Gaelic oral culture). The bardic persona also has to be seen against the background of the age of sentiment and sensibility that reacted against the polished urbanity in wit and expression that characterized the earlier eighteenth century, most especially in the poetic circle of Alexander Pope. Part of the reaction against Augustan urbanity in the age of sensibility comprised a return to the rural locus. The vogue for bucolic poetry, drawing upon ancient pastoral techniques but with a greater focus upon the common folk and their mores realistically delineated, was a long-standing eighteenth-century British literary project collaborated in by such as John Gay and Allan Ramsay, and was later brought to a height of contemplative and didactic sophistication by the likes of Oliver Goldsmith and Thomas Gray. (Burns draws from the latter an epigraph to his most expansive painting of the rural scene in 'The Cotter's Saturday Night', one of the showpieces most

14

admired by the poet's contemporaries in the Kilmarnock edition.)

In the Kilmarnock edition Burns locates himself within a fairly wide-ranging rural context. 'The Cotter's Saturday Night' is a piece of high didacticism, and an exercise in the sublime, extolling virtuous simplicity, and 'The Death and Dying Words of Poor Mailie' and its companion piece, 'Poor Mailie's Elegy', are at the other end of the spectrum in their whimsical, comical effect. 'The Holy Fair', 'Address to the Deil' and 'Halloween' are all reflections upon the 'folk' culture of rural Ayrshire, though with a strong anthropological analysis that belongs more than anything else to the intellectual currents of the Enlightenment. Three poems mark the poet's seemingly most intense engagement with rural 'objects'. 'The Auld Farmer's New-year-morning Salutation to His Auld Mare, Maggie' has a serious side to it in essaying a close identification between the farmer and his horse, and so looks, in proto-Romantic fashion, towards the communion of man and nature. 'To a Mouse' performs a similar manoeuvre, but contains within it a political allegory in response to the rapid agrarian change of the late eighteenth century. 'To a Mountain-Daisy' (*PS* 92) marks one of Burns's most extreme exercises in rural sentiment as he identifies the wind-blown flower with the fragility of his own poetic naivety:

> Such is the fate of simple Bard,
> On Life's rough ocean luckless starr'd!
> Unskilful he to note the card
>   Of *prudent Lore*,
> Till billows rage, and gales blow hard,
>   And whelm him o'er!
>
> (ll. 37–42)

Critics have generally disliked 'To a Mountain-Daisy' and it is difficult to defend Burns here from the charge of precious preening, as the poem drowns in *King Lear*-soaked pathetic fallacy.

Burns's most extended piece attempting to define his poetic location is 'The Vision' (*PS* 62), a poem that has found little critical favour, but which is, arguably, the most ambitious creative experiment in the Kilmarnock edition. Written in the 'Habbie' stanza, it is structured around two cantos, or 'Duans' (a

15

term of division borrowed from Macpherson's Ossianic text 'Cath-Loda'), and attempts a landscape-surveying didacticism of the kind that was made so popular in the eighteenth century by the Anglo-Scot James Thomson. In Scottish terms, then, we have Burns assembling disparate elements: the stanza of the Scots poetry revival, 'Celtic' Scotland and the 'mainstream' British expression (though one arguably charged with Scottish Presbyterian realism) of James Thomson. The title of the poem also recalls Allan Ramsay's text of the same name, a concocted piece of medieval antiquarianism written probably in 1715 out of patriotic complaint lamenting (in its anti-Unionist subtext) that the days of the great Scottish hero William Wallace are gone. Curiously, it is in this most highly synthetic context for a poem that Burns performs his most self-conscious act of identification as a 'simple bard'. 'Duan First' of 'The Vision' sees the narrator worn out with farm labour at the end of the day and demoralized as he contemplates his slender financial means and habitual hunger, and as he berates himself for his unprofitable addiction to writing poetry:

> I started, mutt'ring blockhead! coof!   [fool
> And heav'd on high my wauket loof,   [calloused palm
> To swear by a' yon starry roof,
>   Or some rash aith,   [oath
> That I, henceforth, would be *rhyme-proof*
>   Till my last breath –.

(ll. 31–6)

We should be aware here of the deliberate contradiction written into the poetry as the narrator raises his calloused hand to the sky to swear his oath. There is gentle humour in this juxtaposition of the 'earthy' and the 'starry', but registered also is the indefatigability of the narrator who is clearly not going to simply settle for keeping his attention on the practical, material business of living. Instantly, a figure appears to the narrator, who, in her 'Green, slender, leaf-clad *Holly-boughs*' (l. 49), is a pagan, perhaps Druidic, figure whom the poet rightly takes to be 'some SCOTTISH MUSE' (l. 51). We have a self-reflexive note in keeping with the witty cunning of the text as Burns quotes himself, from his poem, 'To J. S****' (one of several verse epistles where Burns defines his homespun poetic role), as he

16

sees in the woman's expression 'A "hare-brain'd, sentimental trace"' (l. 55). We see something simultaneously mystical and earthy in what follows:

> Down flow'd her robe, a *tartan* sheen,
> Till half a leg was scrimply seen;   [barely
> And such a *leg*! My bonie JEAN
>   Could only peer it;
> Sae straught, sae taper, tight and clean,
>   Nane else came near it.

> Her *Mantle* large, of greenish hue,
> My gazing wonder chiefly drew;
> Deep *lights* and *shades*, bold-mingling, threw
>   A lustre grand;
> And seem'd to my astonish'd view,
>   A *well-known* Land.

(ll. 61–72)

It is the final, revised 'Edinburgh' version of the poem that contains the reference here to Jean Armour, but the Kilmarnock makes reference instead to 'Bess' (Elizabeth Paton, who had borne Burns a daughter in May 1785), and so complicates even further the issue of Burns's fraught personal relationships on the eve of the production of his first book. Whatever the reality of these, there is sly humour (and deep psychological recognition also perhaps) in the narrator's eyeing up in 'The Vision' of the muse who appears to him. The mysterious woman provides him with a vision of the topography of Ayrshire, and, given the family associations of the great patriot with the region, of William Wallace and his warriors driving back the English during the medieval Wars of Independence. Thereafter, this 'Duan' ends with a vision of more contemporary Ayrshire celebrities as we glimpse Lord Barskimming, then lord justice clerk in Scotland, William Fullarton, the agricultural improver, and the mathematician Matthew Stewart and his son, the philosopher Dugald Stewart, who was to become a friend and champion of the poet in his early career (one of the shrewd ploys of 'The Vision' was Burns's clearly successful attempt to extend the patronage available to him). Part of Burns's theme, then, is that if the ancient martial prowess of the Scots is less

17

apparent in his native region, there remain at least the vigour of justice, science and the intellect generally.

At the start of 'Duan Second', the spirit woman salutes the narrator:

> 'All hail! *my own* inspired Bard!
> 'In me thy native Muse regard!
> 'Nor longer mourn thy fate is hard,
> 'Thus poorly low!
> 'I come to give thee such *reward*,
> 'As *we* bestow.'
>
> (ll. 139–44)

This 'reward' is to be assured that he is part of an organic order of beings who practise 'Arts or Arms' (l. 149) within Ayrshire, as the spirit reveals herself to be 'Coila' (or Kyle, the poet's native district). She has been watching over his maturing poetic efforts until now, and he is to be proud of his place within the ranks of poets:

> 'I taught thy manners-painting strains,
> 'The *loves*, the *ways* of simple swains,
> 'Till now, o'er all my wide domains,
> 'Thy fame extends;
> 'And some, the pride of *Coila's* plains,
> 'Become thy friends.
>
> 'Thou canst not learn, nor I can show,
> 'To paint with *Thomson's* landscape-glow;
> 'Or wake the bosom-melting throe,
> 'With *Shenstone's* art;
> 'Or pour, with *Gray*, the moving flow,
> 'Warm on the heart.
>
> 'Yet all beneath th' unrivall'd Rose,
> 'The lowly Daisy sweetly blows;
> 'Tho' large the forest's Monarch throws
> 'His army shade,
> 'Yet green the juicy Hawthorn grows,
> 'Adown the glade.'
>
> (ll. 241–58)

Burns's location now is seen in not only Scottish but also British terms. Earlier, another poet has been named, James Beattie, author of the proto-Romantic *The Minstrel* (1771–4), which follows the formation of a 'natural' poet from the north of Scotland. The narrator of 'The Vision' is somewhat modelling himself on Edwin, the protagonist of Beattie's poem, and given the British fame that the latter work had enjoyed, it might be inferred that Burns here reveals that he had hopes for a wide reception for his published work. Critics have been wont to read a 'national problem' in the name-checking of Shenstone and Gray (as well as Thomson, read essentially as someone who had rid himself of his Scottishness). In 'The Vision', however, Burns shows his awareness of culture as a kind of palimpsest. The beauty of the landscape which inspires him to be a 'Bard' is the only given. Beyond this, cultural history is successively overwritten so that Burns's own region of Kyle has once been a place of a very different language, 'Pictish' (as Burns explains in a note to his poem, the name of Kyle is said ultimately to derive from 'Coilus', king of the Picts); later it is Gaelic-speaking, and the poem refers to the area as being previously part of the demesne of the Campbells and adopts the Ossianic fabric of the 'Duan'; later again we have the Scots-speaking Wallace (though historically French may have been for him a language of greater fluency); and now, in the eighteenth century, Burns's native region is part of a British reality, as he mentions contemporary British parliamentarians and soldiers who hail from Scotland, as well as a very heterogeneous poetic culture (the Scots Thomson and Beattie balancing, in a sense, Shenstone and Gray, both sets of poets having made an impact in mutually 'cross-border' terms). Burns's modesty topos, where he sees himself as a lesser kind of poet, is not without its sly playfulness (as Carol McGuirk observes, we have '*The Seasons* in brief' in the first canto of 'The Vision' contradicting Coilas's later words about the narrator's inability to follow Thomson's lead), but it is also genuine as the narrator realizes the weight of a huge, variegated cultural history which he sits within.[3] He has his place and should confidently occupy this, no matter how complicated the world seems. We should note here that the ultimate belief in 'inspiration' amid the cultural and historical hurly-burly promulgated by 'The Vision' is a harbinger of Romantic poetry (among others, the Wordsworths, Coleridge, Hazlitt and later Byron, Keats and Shelley all see Burns as a watershed moment in British poetry).

The other place in the Kilmarnock edition where Burns is most intent on bardic self-definition is to be found in his verse epistles. In six of these Burns maps out a poetic space for himself and others (Ayrshire poets to whom these works are addressed) where honest, common-sense judgements of the world are allied to the feelings of the heart in response to nature. This, again, demonstrates Burns the cultural transformer. The idea grows up in the Burns cult that Burns's verse epistles are almost his own invention, the appropriate vehicle for his seemingly straightforward expression. However, Burns derives the form principally from his reading of Allan Ramsay, who in many ways is an early eighteenth-century Augustan poet, writing typically in this mode as a marker of his urbanity and civilized wit. Burns's adaptation of the mode, then, for his *non*-urban dialogues is innovative, but his inheritance of the verse epistle should be borne in mind as all too often it has not been in the amnesiac cult that has sought to prioritize the 'heaven-taught ploughman' and to lose sight of Burns the literary craftsman who operates in dialogue with a very wide literary heritage.

'Epistle to Davie, A Brother Poet' (*PS* 51) is addressed to David Sillar, an Irvine grocer and sometime schoolmaster who published his poems in Scots in 1789, like so many others following Burns's lead. Of the several local poets that Burns praises in various verse epistles in the Kilmarnock edition, all are mediocre as Burns must have known. These individuals were men with whom he socialized, but it is not merely out of friendship that he salutes them: we see Burns marking out a wider, more legitimate space for himself in presenting himself as part of a poetic grouping in rural, Presbyterian Ayrshire. 'Epistle to Davie' utilizes a stanza form taken from 'The Cherrie and the Slae' by the great Catholic Ayrshire poet of the seventeenth century, Alexander Montgomerie. Burns's poem is supposed to hymn simple poetic resources, but here we see that he is again an archaeologist, retrieving a form that he encountered in printings of Montgomerie by James Watson and Allan Ramsay (who also used the stanza in his own original work), and reviving it as a third 'Scottish' stanza overlooked by Robert Fergusson. Burns's verse epistle is a recommendation to enjoy the natural environment and simple human health and emotions. It is one of his poems that cement Burns's reputation as a poet of nature:

It's no in titles nor in rank;
It's no in wealth like *Lon'on Bank*,
  To purchase peace and rest;
It's no in makin muckle, *mair*:   [plenty; more
It's no in books; it's no in Lear,   [learning
  To mak us truly blest:
If Happiness hae not her seat
  And center in the breast,
We may be *wise*, or *rich*, or *great*,
  But never can be *blest*:
    Nae treasures, nor pleasures
      Could make us happy lang;
    The *heart* ay's the part ay,   [always
      That makes us right or wrang.

(ll. 57–70)

Burns is here again the child of the age of sensibility (in other words we see him belonging in the mainstream of British literary culture on the eve of the Romantic movement), even though, ironically, this impetus is somewhat misread in his own community as emanating simply from his marginal Ayrshire locus. In his final stanza the poet reflects on the name of his lover 'Jean' (one of his unbought 'treasures' and 'pleasures', and the irony is replete, given the uncertainty of who is to be 'named' Burns's true love in the Kilmarnock edition):

O, how that *name* inspires my style!
The words come skelpan, rank and file,   [thrashing
  Amaist before I ken!
The ready measure rins as fine,
As *Phœbus* and the famous *Nine*
  Were glowran owre my pen.
My spavet *Pegasus* will limp,   [tumoured on the shank
  Till ance he's fairly het;   [hot
And then he'll hilch, and stilt, and jimp, [lurch; prance; jump
  And rin an unco fit: [strange foot
    But least then, the beast then,
      Should rue his hasty ride,
    I'll light now, and dight now,   [wipe clean
      His sweaty, wizen'd hide.

(ll. 141–54)

Burns's 'spavet' (a spavin is a tumour interfering with a horse's shank) Pegasus is not the winged horse associated with the

21

Muses, but an overworked plough-horse. Humorously here, Burns refers to himself and his own travails labouring on his farm, and, of course, the deft movement of the stanza belying the idea of limping, forms a modesty topos that, like most such topoi, is not to be taken seriously. The poet's knowledge of Pegasus and the nine Muses (to say nothing of his usage of a received stanza-form) also contradicts the alleged primitivism of the poem, but this again shows the increasing emphasis upon sheer inspiration in the British literary mainstream as learned men (such as Burns) mould the energies of the proto-Romantic age. Burns's construction of his bardic image, it would be fair to say, is sometimes playful in its contradictory stance and in poems such as 'The Vision' and 'Epistle to Davie' essays a fissured terrain between the ages of neoclassicism and Romanticism. More unsatisfactory than such problematic 'bardic' location are occasional moments where Burns is all too smugly serious and too summative of his supposedly instinctual bardic nature. In the final poem in the Kilmarnock edition, 'A Bard's Epitaph' (PS 104), Burns projects on to his own notional demise a didacticism that both warns against excessively following primitive instincts and cloyingly exhorts sympathy for his misjudgements:

> Is there a man whose judgement clear,
> Can others teach the course to steer,
> Yet runs, himself, life's mad career,
> > Wild as the wave,
> Here pause – and thro' the starting tear,
> > Survey his grave.

> The poor Inhabitant below
> Was quick to learn and wise to know,
> And keenly felt the friendly glow,
> > And *softer flame*;
> But thoughtless follies laid him low,
> > And stain'd his name!

> > > (ll. 13–24)

How can Burns expect such lines to be taken seriously, since in being able to write them (that is to say, he is not yet dead) it is surely not too late to avoid the full effects of the 'follies' to which he refers? Burns here is a poseur, an all-too-transparent 'man of feeling' attempting to justify his life (including, presumably, those facets of it which are troubling him as the 'Kilmarnock' goes into production) with recourse to his calling as a man of instinctive (bardic) passion. Burns, indeed, demonstrates here, even as he attempts to inhabit a moral discourse, a thinly disguised moral exceptionalism that is to be the mark of so many writers from the Romantic age onwards.

Ironically, 'A Bard's Epitaph' turns out to be extraordinarily prescient of Burns's posthumous fame where he is so often taken to be an exemplum of immorality. This subsumption of his life and work into a seemingly straightforward story (here a morality tale) is something to which popular Burnsian biography is all too prone. In fact, the resistance actually deep within his work to easy definition, the reality that he is so culturally trammelled, makes Burns one of the most interesting of writers in the entire canon of Scottish, British and, perhaps, world literature. Time and again the 'officially' received Burns is one that underplays his creative amplitude, and we see this in the initial and long-enduring response to the Kilmarnock edition, which hails him, typically, as a local rural writer of some comic and even satiric observation, but of an essential decency (to be completely assured with the shaving off of a few rough edges). We see this in the views of the Edinburgh professor Hugh Blair, who sought to purge Burns's poems of what he took to be sexual crudity, and in the preface to the slightly expanded Edinburgh edition of *Poems, Chiefly in the Scottish Dialect* produced in 1787 that assured Burns's status as a literary phenomenon. Where the Kilmarnock edition had comprised 600 copies subscribed to by no more than a dozen principal worthies, the subscriber list to the Edinburgh edition ran to over 1300 names and sold in its initial two runs over 3000 copies, bringing Burns a saturation readership among both the intelligentsia and aristocracy of Scotland. The poet writes in his preface:

> Though much indebted to your goodness, I do not approach you, my Lords and Gentlemen, in the usual stile of dedication, to thank you for past favours; that path is so hackneyed by prostituted Learning, that honest Rusticity is ashamed of it. – Nor do I present this Address with the venal soul of a servile Author, looking for a continuation of those favours: I was bred to the Plough, and am independent. I come to claim the common Scottish name with you,

my illustrious Countrymen; and to tell the world that I glory in the title. – I come to congratulate my Country, that the blood of her ancient heroes still runs uncontaminated; and that from your courage, knowledge, and public spirit, she may expect protection, wealth and liberty. – In the last place, I come to proffer my warmest wishes to the Great Fountain of Honour, the Monarch of the Universe, for your welfare and happiness.[4]

Here is a very different Burns from that found in his artful preface to the Kilmarnock edition. Emphasizing his religious bent, his morality and, most ironically, his independence from patronage and the usual hankering after literary fame, Burns is playing exactly the game that his subscribers want. Having arrived in the Scottish capital to superintend the publication of the Edinburgh edition, Burns may yet have felt insecure as to his long-term viability as a poet, since he effectively sold his rights to his poems to his publisher, the sly William Creech, for 100 guineas. Burns's Edinburgh preface, then, might be read as the poet consciously attempting to maximize his short-term returns, but, at the same time, he had somewhat locked himself into an official 'bardic' role which, as we shall see, was often far narrower than the genuinely alternative energies which emanated from the poet.

3

Religion

A powerful populist notion of Burns as a pious Presbyterian poet developed during the nineteenth century. Although this myth blatantly ignored awkward aspects of the poet's life and work concerning his attitudes to morality and his satirizing of Scottish Protestantism, it is not entirely without substance. In 1794 Burns wrote the following lines on the Solemn League and Covenant of 1643, which was both the attempt by the Scottish Covenanters to impose a Presbyterian system of church government on England and Ireland as well as Scotland, and a document that sought also to set limitations upon crown interference in matters of religious confession:

> The Solemn League and Covenant
> Now brings a smile, now brings a tear.
> But sacred Freedom, too, was theirs;
> If thou 'rt a slave, indulge thy sneer.

> (*PS* 512)

Burns's sentiments here have to be read against post-Enlightenment and post-1789 sensibilities. The Enlightenment historiographical tradition, which was particularly strong in Scotland (found most famously in the work of David Hume), had berated in general terms the tendency towards 'fanaticism' in European history. The bloody, internecine disputes of the British seventeenth century, therefore, were to be frowned upon. However, another movement in tandem with this 'civilized' historiographical impulse of the Enlightenment was to be found in its interest in understanding psychology. The stadialist impulse found in Scottish commentators such as Adam Ferguson, where the mentality of a culture was estimated in accordance with its stage of development as a society, began to extend a measure of objective understanding to earlier, more 'primitive' ages in

25

history. And this effect was compounded by universalist Enlightenment theories of morality. If the most celebrated European version of the latter was to be found in Rousseau's idea of the 'noble savage', Scotland had its own influential eighteenth-century tradition of a 'moral sense' innate to humanity and essentially unchanged by cultural or historical location, as described by Presbyterian philosopher Francis Hutcheson. It is against this background that we must understand Burns's retrieval of the previously presumed 'fanatical' Scottish Covenanters, whose core impetus, notwithstanding its somewhat severe doctrinal dressing, was the universal desire for 'Freedom'. We glimpse in the lines by Burns above both a 'Scottish' project and also a wider British Whig project where, following the recent centenary celebrations of the 'Glorious Revolution' of 1688–9 in Britain, and the consonantly chiming occurrence of the French Revolution of 1789, Protestant dissenters of the seventeenth century are re-read as prophets of a more enlightened constitutional democracy in Britain and France.

Burns's ambidexterity, though, must also be acknowledged. If in the lines above he is a sincere mouthpiece for the Scottish Protestant dissenting tradition, he can also be found in very different colours elsewhere. A strikingly different doctrinal expression is to be found in Burns in April 1791 as he sends to the elderly Jacobite and Catholic Lady Winifred Maxwell Constable his song 'Lament of Mary Queen of Scots on the Approach of Spring', in response to the lady's gift to the poet of a snuffbox which was inlaid with a miniature of Mary. Burns writes to Lady Winifred of this present:

> I shall set it apart: the symbols of Religion shall only be more sacred. – In the moment of Poetic composition, the Box shall be my inspiring Genius. – When I would breathe the comprehensive wish of Benevolence for the happiness of others, I shall recollect Your Ladyship; when I would interest my fancy in the distresses incident to Humanity, I shall remember the unfortunate Mary. (L ii. 88–9)

Although there is here a little gentle, Alexander Pope-like, zeugmatic humour with regard to the notion of breathing 'Benevolence' as well as snuff from a snuffbox, the overall tenor of Burns's expression is sincere. Burns clearly writes in the inflexions of Catholic piety. His insertion of a poem that invites

26

sympathy as it speaks in the persona of Mary, a woman previously seen by most Scots as the last word in dark, feminine, papist despotism, is a striking ecumenical manoeuvre on the part of one from Burns's religious background. For all that Burns might be seen simply as a typically temperamental writer in his ability to celebrate, at different times, both Covenanters and Mary, there is a more satisfactory answer to the puzzle of his promiscuous identification with such disparate individuals. On the one hand Burns has available to him the work of the Scottish Enlightenment historian William Tytler of Woodhouselee, who had recently rehabilitated Mary as a figure of some admirable personal and political attributes. On the other, he was also aware of the work of other historians, such as John Howie, contemporaneously doing a similar job in the late eighteenth century for Protestant figures of the Scottish Reformation and seventeenth century. In short, the late eighteenth century in Scotland is a place where Scots begin to survey their pluralistic historical heritage along less inflexibly partial confessional lines and to find objective worth in what were previously seen as darker corners of the nation's past.

Burns's own literary career reflects the increasingly open attitude towards religious identity in late eighteenth-century Scotland. During the late 1770s he is the author of simultaneously dour and lachrymose works of piety, which speak of a rather unforgiving type of Presbyterian and Calvinist sensibility. This is a very different Burns from the one who, in a letter of November 1787, intimates to his confidante, Mrs Dunlop, that the finest religious figure he has ever met is the cultured Catholic bishop John Geddes. Geddes it is who, in providing the chain of Scottish Catholic seminaries and monasteries abroad with copies of the Edinburgh edition, is one of the first to promote Burns's work on the continent. Burns's early religious poetry, in keeping with its production during a miserable part of the poet's life in Irvine during 1781 as an apprentice flax-dresser, sees him full of worldly angst. 'To Ruin' (*PS* 12) features a speaker hailing the 'inexorable lord' (l. 1) submitting to the inevitability of death and even willing his own demise. What is also glimpsed here, however, is not simply Burns's own somewhat puritanical Protestant back-ground, but eighteenth-century literary fashion as well. If the bleak note in this poem is an authentic register of the religion in which he had been raised since a child, the wallowing in the physicality of death is a product also of the huge popularity of Edward Young's *Night Thoughts* (1742–5) and other works Burns consumed, such as Henry Mackenzie's *The Man of Feeling* (1771), that were influential in driving the 'age of sentiment'. He addresses death thus:

> No fear more, no tear more,
> To stain my lifeless face,
> Enclasped, and grasped,
> Within thy cold embrace!

(ll. 25–9)

Lines such as these in an ostensibly religious poem fit all too appositely alongside Burns's infamous remark in 1783 that Mackenzie's emotion-wringing novel was for him 'a book I prize next to the Bible' (*L* i. 17). There are, however, moments of spiritual questing in his poetry of this period, less mediated by his secular literary tastes, and where we see a young man trying to make sense of his tendency to enjoy life in the face of the disapproving god of his ancestors and identifying God-appointed human nature as contradictory. For instance in 'A Prayer, in the Prospect of Death' (*PS* 13), at a moment of illness in Irvine where he seems genuinely to have feared that his end might be nigh, he confesses:

> Thou know'st that Thou hast formed me,
> With Passions wild and strong;
> And list'ning to their witching voice
> Has often led me wrong.

(ll. 9–12)

In this period Burns also tries his hand at psalmody, where he seems to find a less remote God:

> O THOU, the first, the greatest friend
> Of all the human race!
> Whose strong right hand has ever been
> Their stay and dwelling-place!

(*PS* 20, ll. 1–4)

As J. Walter McGinty has claimed, there is a gentle, contemplative quality in this piece that interprets the first six verses of the ninetieth psalm, which makes it appear 'a personal declaration

28

of faith'.[1] Here and in another contemporary piece, 'Remorse' (*PS* 26), Burns clearly shows himself to be a moderate or 'new licht' Presbyterian, of the kind that emphasized conscience rather than grace and a benevolent rather than an awful God. This type of Presbyterian slowly began to occupy the intellectual high-ground following the Scottish Enlightenment, and Burns explicitly filters religious orthodoxy through Enlightenment philosophy in 'Remorse' where he cites Adam Smith's concept of 'sympathy' in a headnote to the poem, and explains that hell itself is the 'tort'ring, gnawing consciousness of guilt' (l. 10) in having done wrong to others.

Of Burns's early contemplative writing on religion, the Kilmarnock edition gathers up only 'To Ruin' and 'A Prayer, in the Prospect of Death' which are included in a section of half a dozen poems that showcase Burns's pessimistic register, generally, rather than his religious sensibility per se. Of these pieces, the song 'Man Was Made to Mourn, A Dirge' (*PS* 64) is interesting in putting forth a title that looks primed by the orthodox Calvinist *contemptus mundi* outlook, but is rather more bitter, implicitly, than accepting in the face of the disappointments of the world. In a letter of 16 August 1788, Burns writes to Mrs Dunlop associating this piece with 'the neglected Many, whose nerves, whose sinews, whose days, whose thoughts, whose independence, whose peace, nay, whose very gratifications & enjoyments, the instinctive gift of Nature, are sacrificed & sold to these few bloated Minions of Heaven!' (*L* i. 306). Burns here makes explicit the class critique that is certainly there in the song, but which is understated even as it finds a less than wholly orthodox consolation in the grave:

> O Death! the poor man's dearest friend,
> ....
> The Great, the Wealthy fear thy blow,
>   From pomp and pleasure torn;
> But Oh! a blest relief to those
>   That weary-laden mourn!

(ll. 81 and 85–8)

Burns seems to be understandably careful in the Kilmarnock edition not to offend too far against political or religious propriety, and this suggests that he had a good conceit of his own abilities and knew that there was a strong chance of his book coming to a wide and mainstream notice in late eighteenth-century Scottish society. Later feigned surprise at his work's popularity rings hollow from the poet. The shrewdness of his choices of material (and the repression of the fully-flexed thinking that he reveals to Mrs Dunlop) for his first publication belie his innocent, bardic self-image, even as, paradoxically, these choices are designed to cement the perception of him as a child of nature not all that interested in the workings of the human world. There is no shrewder choice than 'The Cotter's Saturday Night' (PS 72), the poem that of all the material in Burns's opening oeuvre attracts the largest approbation from the mainstream Scottish literati. Robert Heron strikes a keynote in the proud (Scottish) national response to the poem when he says that it 'is really a faithful description from the life, [and] proves that the manners of our rustics can afford subjects for pastoral poetry more elevated and more amiable than those which are exhibited in Gay's "Shepherd's Week"'.[2] It is 'The Cotter's Saturday Night' that has allowed, almost down to the present day, the flawed insistence on Burns as, underneath all else, a man of deeply pious Protestant inclination. If twentieth-century Burns criticism gradually offered a corrective to the idea of the poem's authenticity both as a piece of simple realism, or 'natural literature', and as an index of Burns's true belief system, it has arguably gone too far, however, in discounting the serious cultural project that Burns undertakes in this poem.

'The Cotter's Saturday Night' relates to Burns's biography in being, like a number of his early poems, a sincere tribute to his father, William, who had died in 1784 (though William was a tenant farmer, slightly higher up the class ladder than a 'cotter'). Burns felt both guilt and gratitude towards his father. Burns's father had composed for Robert and his brother Gilbert a small instructional handbook, *A Manual of Religious Belief in Dialogue between Father and Son* (written c.1765). Burns's father was, to some extent, a traditional Calvinist, as is seen in disapproving of Robert taking dancing lessons, but he was far from being immune to the new religious emphasis among his communion by the second half of the eighteenth century, and in this manual the ideas of following the love that is in one's heart and of a benevolent God are to the fore. Burns's affectionate remembrance of his father grew out of his consciousness also that in his typically Presbyterian prioritizing of education, William had brought Robert and Gilbert, in effect, a private tutor in the person of John Murdoch, who periodically lived with the Burnes family and introduced Robert to a fairly wide range of the best British literature. As if this were not enough, William's near bankruptcy as he struggled with increasing demands made upon tenant farmers by rapacious landlords during the late eighteenth century, and his eventual death, worn out by farm labour and anxiety, rightly made him in his son's eyes a figure of huge moral stature. 'The Cotter's Saturday Night' depicts a grave dignity in 'the toil-worn COTTER' (l. 14), as, at the end of his working week and to usher in the Sabbath, he gathers around him his family and servants to praise their maker. In the poem the Cotter is implicitly compared both to wise Old Testament patriarch and to a suffering, forbearing, loving Christ-figure as he reads from Scripture. Burns presents a portrait of a figure who is practically engaged in this world, but whose engagements are enmeshed in his awareness of a higher sphere:

> Then kneeling down to HEAVEN'S ETERNAL KING,
>   The *Saint*, the *Father*, and the *Husband* prays:
> Hope 'springs exulting on triumphant wing,'
>   That thus they all shall meet in future days:
> There, ever bask in *uncreated rays*,
>   No more to sigh, or shed the bitter tear,
> *Together* hymning their CREATOR'S praise
>   In *such society*, yet still more dear;
> While circling Time moves round in eternal sphere.
>
>   (ll. 136–44)

Burns shows himself as part of the British dissenting mentality of the late eighteenth century, an outlook increasingly confident as it more frequently wields literature in its service. We see a Burns who is close in attitude to his contemporaries Blake and Coleridge as he invests in the simpler forms of Protestant worship a truer form of priesthood:

> Compar'd with this, how poor Religion's pride,
>   In all the pomp of *method*, and of *art*,
> When men display to congregations wide,
>   Devotion's ev'ry grace, except the *heart*!
> The POWER, incens'd, the Pageant will desert,
>   The pompous strain, the sacerdotal stole;

But haply, in some *Cottage* far apart,
    May hear, well pleas'd, the language of the *Soul*;
    And in His *Book of Life* the Inmates poor enroll.

(ll. 145–53)

The dedication of 'The Cotter's Saturday Night' reveals it to be one of the cornerstones of the Kilmarnock edition. This is to the lawyer Robert Aiken, the earliest encourager of Burns's pre-published work as the poet read it aloud among their circle of professional friends around Ayr and Alloway, the man who personally collected almost a quarter of the subscribers that facilitated the publishing of the Kilmarnock volume and a person that Burns hails as 'Dear Patron of my Virgin Muse' (*L* i. 72). The poem, then, is not only a repayment to William Burnes, but an act of gratitude also to that society of upwardly mobile, clubbable cultured young men of which Burns's father did not entirely approve. In the opening stanza the poet addresses Aiken, 'To you I sing, in simple Scottish lays' (l. 5), and says that his friend is going to hear of the life of the cotter into which had he been born Aiken would have been happier. Burns is not here being humorous but is referring to the travails of the law which brought Aiken into such close proximity with human depravity (there is, however, something of an ironic intertextuality between this poem and another contemporary piece by Burns, given Aiken's involvement in the Presbyterian politics of the real-life events that inspired 'Holy Willie's Prayer').

Less easily taken at face value by criticism is Burns's claim to be peddling 'simple Scottish lays', as 'The Cotter's Saturday Night' is a poem that, in fact, reveals an instance of Robert Crawford's 'British Burns'.[3] It is prefaced by lines from Thomas Gray's 'Elegy Written in a Country Churchyard' that recommend a simple, pastoral, quietest life. Burns's poem is also written in the Spenserian stanza, a vehicle that was channelled through the eighteenth century by the English poets Matthew Prior and William Shenstone and by the 'Anglo-Scots' James Thomson and James Beattie. In both moral tone and form, then, Burns has embarked on a thoroughly mainstream mode of Augustan didacticism. At the same time, however, one should be aware of the 'Scottish' nuances at work in the poem. More generally, it should be acknowledged that the legacy of Edmund Spenser (like that of John Milton, to whom Burns makes

32

frequent reference in his work) is seen in Burns's time as part of the common British Protestant heritage in which Scots from a Presbyterian background glory, with no vexed 'national' question complicating this identification.

More particularly, Burns's thematic and stanzaic impetuses in 'The Cotter's Saturday Night' are most directly derived from Robert Fergusson's 'The Farmer's Ingle' (1773). Fergusson's use of the stanza here is interesting, given that he is essentially hostile to Presbyterian or 'Whiggish' Scottish culture. A crypto-Jacobite whose cultural allegiances are primarily to an Episcopalian and even a Catholic literary canon within Scotland, Fergusson wilfully appropriates the Spenserian stanza. He uses it to celebrate a peasantry which laughs at the 'cutty-stool' and the strictures of the national Scottish church, secure as they are in their bucolic lifestyle, a hard existence but containing good simple food and alcohol and unlicensed sexuality, and which continues to acknowledge folk traditions, including songs and tales of ghosts (both things that would be theologically problematic to the most orthodox of Presbyterians down to the time of Burns). In Fergusson's poetry, generally, work being written only a decade before that of Burns, there would be no question of celebrating the Presbyterian figure, a constant source of ridicule for men of Fergusson's outlook. Burns, however, can be seen again in his ambidexterity as he draws upon Fergusson, a poet who more than any other determines the tone, themes and modes of a large part of Burns's work, and simultaneously upon an Enlightenment mentality that will extend to men of his father's background some necessary understanding and even veneration.

'The Cotter's Saturday Night', then, as Burns adapts materials from Fergusson's work is, like 'The Vision', an act of cultural transformation. Burns in his poem provides a measure of rehabilitation for the Presbyterian patriarch, made necessary by his awareness of the long-standing stereotype of the dour, fanatically religious Scot, promulgated by a wide set of prejudice – Scottish as well as English, and here we might recall Tobias Smollett's portrait, albeit of subtle nuance, of such an individual in his morose, canting Lismahago in *The Expedition of Humphry Clinker* (1771), a character hugely enjoyed during the later eighteenth century, especially by its southern audience. Burns also borrows from Fergusson's poem the idea of the commendably simple sustenance of the peasantry. Fergusson's poem had couched in terms of quasi-communion the basic fare of the country folk (this is the ultimate source of Burns's flippant treatment of the same in his 'To a Haggis'), but Burns changes the theological tenor of this idea more in keeping with Presbyterian thinking, picturing the Word (rather than the symbol of supper) as the sacred communitarian glue. Summing up the Saturday night piety, the poet says, 'From Scenes like these, old SCOTIA'S grandeur springs' (l. 163), and he goes on to rail against that ubiquitous eighteenth-century vice, 'luxury' (l. 177), as he pictures in the Scottish peasantry: 'A *virtuous Populace* [that] may rise the while, / And stand a wall of fire, around their much-lov'd ISLE' (ll. 179–80). Seemingly contradicting the 'British' frame of reference in the line just cited, however, Burns's final stanza hymns the great champion of Scottish independence, William Wallace.

In its mode and in its attitude to 'nation', 'The Cotter's Saturday Night' has been read by some critics as contradictory and confused. Truly, it is an assemblage as we see in its largely mainstream Augustan English cadences smattered occasionally and inconsistently with Scots phraseology, and also in one stanza (ll. 55–63) which expresses a less than convincing wide-eyed horror at the idea of the attempted seduction of a simple Scots peasant-lass by a 'rake', a scenario imported straight from the most melodramatic novels of the time. Overall, however, the poem is an exciting experiment demonstrating Burns's bi-cultural 'British' facility which was certainly successful in conveying to a wider audience a more admirable portrait of Scottish Presbyterianism (among the poem's admirers was to be numbered, for instance, Coleridge). It is also tellingly expansive in its treatment of national identity. We see this as Burns, in adapting Fergusson's model, brings Presbyterian identity in from the literary cold in Scotland and as he suggests that the ancient British myths of liberty and (island) independence – so powerful throughout the eighteenth-century British political vocabulary in opposition to what these myths took to be truly foreign (because despotic and imperial) powers such as Spain and France – are to be associated with William Wallace (certainly no hero in English legend) as much as with any great English champion of the same values. 'The Cotter's Saturday Night', then, is a very composite work in its materials, but is an

34

intelligent experiment in bringing together a range of cultural impetuses to which Burns was heir, and to which he stood in a relationship of general approbation.

The Kilmarnock and the Edinburgh editions show Burns gradually increasing the strain of Calvinist satire which had been a more prominent approach to his religious background prior to its celebration in 'The Cotter's Saturday Night'. The most ferocious piece in this regard is 'Holy Willie's Prayer', written in early 1785, which was an important component in the formation of Burns's early reputation. In one of the poet's keynote statements about his art, his letter to Dr John Moore of August 1787, Burns describes the local popularity with which his 'The Holy Fair' met when he passed it around his neighbourhood in manuscript, and the infamy engendered by 'Holy Willie's Prayer' that followed it: 'With a certain side of both clergy and laity it met with a roar of applause. – Holy Willie's Prayer next made its appearance, and alarmed the kirk-Session so much that they held three several meetings to look over their holy artillery, if any of it was pointed against profane Rhymers' (L i. 144). In spite of the poet's levity here over the reception of the second poem it clearly had an effect, since only the first of these pieces made it into the two contemporary editions of Burns's work. The Kilmarnock edition publishes a short 'epitaph' 'On a Celebrated Ruling Elder', but this is as far as Burns dares go in portraying the rabid hypocrisy of the Calvinist mentality that he paints so deeply in 'Holy Willie's Prayer'. That poem becomes part of Burns's reserved canon. He is certainly proud of the piece, sending fair copies of it to several correspondents, but in his lifetime it is only published by others, anonymously and in pamphlet form, and does not find its way into editions of Burns's collected works until 1818. In spite of the increasingly moderate Presbyterianism following on from the Enlightenment, religious sensibility remained a delicate quantity in Scotland as is shown by the fact that the Church of Scotland minister and celebrated man of letters Hugh Blair suggested to the poet that he even tone down his comments on Scottish religion between the Kilmarnock and the Edinburgh editions, since some of these gave 'offence'.[4]

'The Holy Fair' (PS 70), like 'The Cotter's Saturday Night', sees Burns also imbibing the influence and adapting the materials of

Robert Fergusson, particularly his 'Hallow-Fair' (1772) and 'Leith Races' (1773). Like Fergusson's poems, it is written in the 'Christ's Kirk' stanza, a vehicle that comes increasingly to be associated during the eighteenth century with carnivalesque celebration in Scotland. It is Burns's distinctive adaptation, however, to make a Presbyterian religious gathering the occasion for such poetic 'celebration'. Describing an Ayrshire field-gathering where in summertime Presbyterians would congregate to partake of (a standard annual) communion and to hear a number of sermons, the poem clearly has some basis in reality. It is, however, like 'The Cotter's Saturday Night', another cultural assemblage. The 'Christ's Kirk' stanza form was, like so much of the formal paraphernalia of the Scots poetry revival of the eighteenth century, an indicator of the festive, anti-puritanical outlook that Ramsay, Fergusson and others adopted in the face of a Presbyterian – and so what they took to be a culturally denuded – Scotland. Burns, then, is performing a feat of cultural engineering in bringing this mode with its indulgent portrayal of the human appetites to bear on a Presbyterian 'festival'. Crucially, also, while 'The Holy Fair' is, indeed, a satire it is not simply a satire but extends to the common folk, at least, at the field meeting a large measure of understanding and even affection.

'The Holy Fair' begins with the narrator walking on a glorious summer morning and encountering three women (a number that humorously plays with the connotations that they might be witches). The three, though, are not all similar allegorical figures in being 'Superstition', 'Hypocrisy' and 'Fun' (the first two in their sour demeanour and black dress being Calvinists). Fun tells the narrator that they are all going to a 'holy fair' (l. 41), a term that Burns footnotes to his poem as 'a common phrase in the West of Scotland for a sacramental occasion'. It is far from clear, however, whether or not this coinage was in widespread common parlance before Burns's poem so popularized it. We should be careful of Burns's craftiness here as an 'inventor' of cultural space, since the phrase so chimes with the paradoxical psychology and language that the poet promulgates so adeptly in the text. In other words, arguably, in insisting on the real-life usage of the phrase, Burns is attempting to validate as simple realism his own particular (highly imaginative) perspective upon the Presbyterian mentality. It is somewhat ironic, then, that a widespread attitude within the Burns cult has been the one-dimensional view that Burns essentially is a realist, more or less simply portraying the scenes and bringing out the innate attitudes of his Ayrshire background, something that downplays Burns's frequent playfulness. Slyly on the part of the poem, the narrator is invited to the fair by fun, rather than the two Calvinist-types, and he agrees to go. The scene that confronts the narrator when he arrives at the meeting-place is one of normal, excited, human, secular life:

Here, farmers gash, in ridin graith,	[dress
Gaed hoddan by their cotters;	[jogging
There, swankies young, in braw braid-claith,	[healthy or
	strapping individuals
Are springan owre the gutters.	
The lasses, skelpan barefit, thrang,	[throng
In silks an' scarlets glitter;	
Wi' *sweet-milk cheese*, in mony a whang,	[thick slice
An' *farls*, bak'd wi' butter,	[bannocks
Fu' crump that day.	[baked dry/well

(ll. 55–63)

Throughout the poem there is an emphasis upon the physical reality of human life and the spiritual motivation for the gathering is ironically but appositely relegated to sideshow entertainment as different ministers of the gospel offer a range of styles to be sampled. One 'auld licht', or traditional Calvinist, preacher unwittingly exemplifies the core of his faith that humanity is fallen and bestial:

Hear how he clears the points o' Faith
Wi' rattlin an' thumpin!
Now meekly calm, now wild in wrath,
He's stampan, an' he's jumpan!
His lengthen'd chin, his turn'd up snout,
His eldritch squeel an' gestures,   [uncanny
O how they fire the heart devout,
Like cantharidian plaisters
On sic a day!

(ll. 109–17)

The freakish orator becomes porcine, and so implicitly devilish (he has a 'snout' and he 'squeels' in an 'eldritch' or 'uncanny' fashion) in the fervour of his own performance, and his effect is like an aphrodisiac (in the reference to plasters of cantharides, or 'Spanish fly') on those similarly minded. Here Burns paints extreme religious sensibility as sublimation of the sexual urge, and this forms part of the inverted texture of the poem where, conversely, the ordinary folk of uncomplicated impetus at the gathering are to be swathed, at points, in a sincere religious language:

> O happy is that man, an' blest!
> ....
> Whase ain dear lass, that he likes best
> Comes clinkan down beside him!

(ll. 91 and 93–4)

In a particularly nice moment, a 'new licht' or moderate Presbyterian preacher influenced by the rational principles of the Enlightenment is dismissed as not in keeping with the growing excitement of both the froth of the 'auld licht' fire-sermons and the drinking, eating and flirting throng:

> What signifies his barren shine,
>   Of *moral pow'rs* an' *reason*;
> His English style, an' gesture fine,
>   Are a' clean out o' season.
> Like SOCRATES or ANTONINE,
>   Or some auld pagan heathen,
> The *moral man* he does define,
>   But ne'er a word o' *faith* in
>   That's right that day.

(ll. 127–35)

Here in a sly backhanded 'compliment' to old-time Calvinism – this creed's charged, anti-rational emphasis upon faith is seen, in a sense, as 'natural' since it mirrors the anti-rational enjoyment of the people at the 'fair', and, indeed, unwittingly adds to this carnival-like dispensation. The 'new licht' faith, with its emphasis upon conscience and common or 'moral' sense is out of tenor with the occasion, and very nicely, in yet another of the poem's acts of inversion, these qualities are associated with pre-Christian 'pagans' (such as Socrates). There is no room for the 'moral' man, either in the consumption of religion or the secular shenanigans of this day in late eighteenth-century Ayrshire. The poem maintains its topsy-turvy

38

note until the end, as we are told that 'hearts' and 'flesh' have been pierced in a sense that overrides any supposed results from the Calvinist exhortation to the pure life:

> How monie hearts this day converts,
> O' Sinners and o' Lasses!
> Their hearts o' stane, gin night are gane   [by
> As saft as ony flesh is,
> There's some are fou o' *love divine*;
> There's some are fou o' *brandy*;
> An' monie jobs that day begin,
> May end in *Houghmagandie*   [sexual intercourse
> Some ither day.

(ll. 235–43)

'The Holy Fair' is a poem that draws psychological conclusions as it is implicitly forgiving of human 'frailty' and satirizes Calvinist 'excess' in a way that is of universal appeal. A general critique of the fanatical mindset, it is also part of a corpus of Burns's work which castigates the local church scene in Ayrshire. In his personal morality Burns had come in for public censure from this church, but it is not simply in such experiences that Burns's commentary upon the religious scene of his locality has its genesis. In 'The Twa Dogs' (*PS* 71), one of Burns's best satires on the wider polity of Britain, we are told that the common Presbyterian folk of Scotland, whatever their material circumstances, have a strong sense of their intellectual rights (a legacy of John Knox's emphasis upon parochial education and of the strong lay-involvement by elders and the congregation more widely in the Scottish church), which extends to forthright expression:

> They lay aside their private cares,
> To mind the Kirk an' State affairs;
> They'll talk o' *patronage* an' *priests*,
> Wi' kindling fury i' their breasts.

(ll. 117–20)

In keeping with this mentality, 'The Holy Fair' is full of thinly veiled references to local preachers, and these make this poem part of a corpus in Burns's work. Similarly, 'The Holy Tulzie [brawl]', 'The Ordination' and 'The Kirk of Scotland's Garland – a New Song' (*PS* 264) are all pieces commenting closely upon petty

39

abuses and ridiculous posturing within the Ayrshire church. In the last of these, written in 1789 when Burns is at the height of his cosmopolitan confidence, having travelled widely in Scotland by this time and being just about to embark on a new career as an exciseman, Burns takes his expression a little further. In the form of a political broadside, such as was being increasingly published in the press at this time by those who held pro-reformist politics, 'The Kirk of Scotland's Garland' also sees Burns explicitly inhabiting the anti-clericalism engendered by the French Revolution as he boldly sets himself up in the piece as 'Poet Burns, Poet Burns, wi' your priest-skelping [smacking] turns' (l. 70).

Burns's most celebrated religious satire, 'Holy Willie's Prayer' (*PS* 53), written in 1785, concerns, primarily, the hypocrisy of an elder of the kirk in Mauchline, the real-life William Fisher. In his headnote to the poem Burns reveals his personal animus in the satire since he accuses Fisher, along with the minister William Auld, as standing behind charges upon which Burns's friend Gavin Hamilton was brought before the Presbytery of Ayr. These charges included lack of attendance at his parish church and neglecting family worship, but were eventually dismissed, as Burns tells us, 'owing partly to the oratorical powers of Mr. Robt Aiken, Mr Hamilton's counsel' (given this set of circumstances we have, then, another subtext to 'The Cotter's Saturday Night' dealing with the commendable face of the Presbyterian mentality, and in which Aiken features so prominently). We see here in this set of connections the operation of the 'Ayrshire Enlightenment' in which educated, frequently Masonic individuals such as Burns, Hamilton and Aiken were intent on challenging still-lingering theocratic practices in the name of intellectual and expressive freedom. 'Holy Willie's Prayer' is certainly an act of expressive freedom in being, arguably, one of the greatest ironic monologues in English (or Scots English). Walter Scott, for whom for a lengthy period Burns was the writer he enjoyed more than any other, agreed with James Currie's decision to leave the piece out of the first collected edition of the poet's work since he saw the work as being altogether too vicious, especially in its scatology. Such a judgement, however, overlooks the fact that the poem is an act of psychological sympathy in the widest sense, in reaching inside Holy Willie's mindset and reading it as culturally damaged by identification with the Word in a way that is altogether too personal.

Ostensibly Holy Willie is praying to God, revelling in the majesty of his maker:

> O THOU that in the heavens does dwell!
> Wha, as it pleases best thysel,
> Sends ane to heaven and ten to h-ll,
>   A' for thy glory!
> And no for ony gude or ill
>   They've done before thee.

(ll. 1–6)

Here Willie refers to the most orthodox Calvinist doctrine of predestination, where omniscient God at the beginning of time has looked through human history and has seen or 'decided' who is to be saved and who is to be damned. Willie is pleased that he is one of 'the elect', vouchsafed this knowledge of personal salvation, it would appear, for the simple reason that he has become an elder in the church. His pride swells as he contemplates that God has given him especial favour by not sending him to hell straight away (at a time of more than 70 per cent infant mortality in parts of Britain), as would have been his destination had he died without baptism: 'When from my mother's womb I fell, / Thou might hae plunged me deep in hell' (ll. 19–20). The harsh, unforgiving view of God in extreme Calvinism is thus dissected, and placed alongside this is the attendant egotism of the elected outlook. For Willie, the arbitrary, undeserving nature of any human in the sight of God becomes, paradoxically, a measure of his own special status. The cadences of seeming humility are constantly under-cut in the poem by self-satisfaction:

> What was I, or my generation,
> That I should get such exaltation?
> I, wha deserv'd most just damnation,
>   For broken laws
> Sax thousand years ere my creation,
>   Thro' Adam's cause!

(ll. 13–18)

Willie's views are antediluvian as he shows here his 'knowledge' of the traditional dating of the Earth, views that were beginning

41

to be undermined in 1785 by the published findings of the geologist James Hutton, one of the great scientific figures of the Scottish Enlightenment, whose work Burns was likely to be aware of at this time.

Through an oxymoronic language, more intensely of the sort even than Burns peddles in 'The Holy Fair', we see Willie speaking about himself in the received language of Scripture, though revealing a strong phallic undercurrent to his words:

> Yet I am here, a chosen sample,
> To shew thy grace is great and ample:
> I'm here, a pillar o' thy temple
> > Strong as a rock,
> A guide, a ruler and example
> > To a' thy flock.

(ll. 25–30)

Becoming more and more 'unconscious', Willie asks for forgiveness for his sins of fornication in which he is actually revelling (and, implicitly, in his somewhat stupefied address, our narrator may also be drunk). Willie's 'prayer' becomes, in oxymoronic fashion again, actually a curse as he asks God to bring something horrible down upon the heads of his enemies, Aiken and Hamilton. He refers to his humiliation at their hands:

> O L—d my G-d, that glib-tong'd Aiken!
> My very heart and flesh are quaking
> To think how I sat, sweating, shaking,
> > And p-ss'd wi' dread,
> While Auld wi' hingin lip gaed sneaking
> > And hid his head!

(ll. 85–90)

Thus Willie is ultimately rendered unpleasantly bestial, representing the uncivilized truth of the religious fanatic that Enlightenment intellectuals such as Burns sought to expose.

Burns's attitudes to his native Presbyterian/Calvinist heritage is complex, but in his analysis of this according to the contemporary climate of Enlightenment psychological and historical enquiry, he is a finely nuanced commentator who pierces both unthinking prejudice against his cultural background and is, at the same time, its most lively critic during the eighteenth century.

4

Politics

As Marilyn Butler has claimed, 'Burns's social position and his self-presentation, the [...] traditional language, verse-forms and metres, are all in the end political.'[1] Burns's 'political' construction of himself as a poet, especially as a primitive bard (collaborated in by so many others), or at best an autodidact is, however, not entirely encouraging to the reception of the subtleties in his work. If the notion of Burns as an essentially untutored rustic poet has gradually receded (though it took until well into the nineteenth century before a more 'literary' Burns began to be appreciated), the idea of Burns as a rather one-dimensional ideological or 'party' animal remains. For instance, Burns has been seen, and remains to be seen in much popular mythology, as a somewhat backward looking 'nationalist', a term and a modern political concept to which Burns had no real access. He is, at least, what we would today call a 'cultural nationalist' in adopting the 'Habbie', 'Christ's Kirk' and 'Cherrie and the Slae' stanzas identified with earlier Scots-language poetry, and he can be seen generally, in providing such an ample and successful corpus of poetry in Scots, bucking the trend of linguistic Anglicization that proceeded through Scottish culture in the eighteenth century. He is a 'reviver' also in both writing and collecting several hundred Scots songs (folk songs very often, but including also what one might call 'art songs').

It is also the case that Burns is explicitly a patriotic Scot. In his letter of August 1787 to John Moore he records how reading 'the story of Wallace poured a Scotish prejudice in my veins which will boil along there till the flood-gates of life shut in eternal rest' (*L* i. 136). In November 1786 Burns was delighted to find a request for half a dozen copies of the Kilmarnock edition from Mrs Frances Anna Dunlop, a descendant of the great hero of the

Scottish Wars of Independence. The much older lady from the minor gentry and Burns became great friends and correspondents, and in an early letter to her of 15 January 1787, Burns wrote of wishing to write something in honour of her ancestor: 'My heart glows with a wish to be able to do justice to the merits of the *Saviour of his Country*, which, sooner or later, I shall at least attempt' (*L* i. 85). With one rather mediocre piece, however, 'Gude Wallace', an adaptation of a chapbook ballad, which Burns published in *The Scots Musical Museum* in 1796, Burns came nowhere near fulfilling his stated aim. In his letters to Mrs Dunlop and others, the poet's effusive patriotism seems to be as much a part of his repertoire as a 'man of feeling' as anything else. For instance, on his way to a tour of the Highlands, Burns wrote to Robert Muir from Stirling on 26 August 1787, 'This morning I kneel'd at the tomb of Sir John the Graham, the gallant friend of the immortal WALLACE; and two hours ago, I said a fervent prayer for old Caledonia over the hole in a blue whin-stone where Robert the Bruce fixed his royal Standard on the banks of Bannockburn' (*L* i. 151).

We see here what Kenneth Simpson has identified as the role-playing Burns, as the poet from a Presbyterian background takes on the stance of medieval Catholic piety.[2] Rather, ironically, when Burns does write a great song about the Scottish Wars of Independence, in 1793, it celebrates Robert the Bruce, an icon equivalent to Wallace but historically a much more devious individual who capitalized on Wallace's earlier, more selflessly patriotic work. It may even be that Burns's choice of Bruce here deliberately cocked a snook at Mrs Dunlop, with whom Burns had begun to exchange slightly tense words from late in 1792 over the poet's revolutionary sympathies. Burns's feelings were particularly roused when he considered how the peasant classes had been treated under the *ancien régime* of France, albeit that he was also sympathetic to close relatives of Mrs Dunlop who had had to flee France as the Revolution increasingly purged the aristocratic class. Burns, a full-time crown employee for the excise since September 1791, had to be careful about expressing political sympathies, and his song 'Robert Bruce's March to Bannockburn' (*PS* 425) conveniently lent a historical Scottish alibi to sentiments that were altogether more contemporary in their revolutionary vocabulary:

> Lay the proud Usurpers low!
> Tyrants fall in every foe!
> LIBERTY's in every blow!
> Let us Do – or DIE!!!

(ll. 21–4)

The extract already quoted from Burns's Edinburgh preface shows that this was much more universally 'Scottish' in its emphasis than that of the Kilmarnock preface. Addressing the 'ancient metropolis of Caledonia', the poet was intent on emphasizing the importance of the location of his new, often aristocratic readership. A work written especially for the Edinburgh edition, 'Address to Edinburgh' (*PS* 135), explicitly essays Burns's movement out from a regional to a national focus:

> Edina! *Scotia's* darling seat!
> All hail thy palaces and tow'rs,
> Where once beneath a Monarch's feet,
> Sat Legislation's sov'reign pow'rs!
> From marking wildly-scatt'red flow'rs,
> As on the banks of *Ayr* I stray'd,
> And singing, lone, the ling'ring hours,
> I shelter in thy honor'd shade.

(ll. 1–8)

In the Kilmarnock edition, Burns was rather more content with being the bard of 'Coila', although here already there was the beginning of Burns's 'national project'. Similar to the strategy in 'The Cotter's Saturday Night', 'Scotch Drink' (*PS* 77) lauds the comestible resources of Scotland. This is precisely the kind of performance in which the literati of the day saw Burns's essentially fine nature grappling with a degree of coarseness that they hoped the poet, once better educated, would excise from his work. At points the poem observes a pastoral decorum, where drink has its place as part of a healthy Scots country table:

> On thee aft Scotland chows her cood,   [chews; cud
> In souple scones, the wale o' food!   [supple; choicest
> Or tumbling in the boiling flood
>   Wi' kail an' beef;
> But when thou pours thy strong *heart's blood*,
>   There thou shines chief.

(ll. 19–24)

Elsewhere in the poem, as many of the literati saw it, Burns's enthusiasm led him into vulgarity:

> O *Whisky*! soul o' plays an' pranks!
> Accept a *Bardie's* gratefu' thanks!
> When wanting thee, what tuneless cranks
>   Are my poor Verses!
> Thou comes – they rattle i' their ranks
>   At ither's arses!

(ll. 103–8)

In fact, Burns is a poet who is somewhat iconoclastic or fruitfully assaulting decorum in terms of mixing modes and genre (a tendency that finds its apotheosis in 'Tam o' Shanter'). In 'Scotch Drink' Burns genuinely celebrates a still unfashionable beverage (brandy and wine being altogether more popular in better Scottish society at this time), but does so largely with disarming comedy, assaulting the prejudice against whisky as he suggests that rival tipples are examples of false refinement in Scotland (a trick he replicates in the realm of food in 'To a Haggis', added in the Edinburgh edition).

Burns's theme is drink again in the next poem in the Kilmarnock edition, 'The Author's Earnest Cry and Prayer, to the Right Honorable and Honorable, the Scotch Representatives in the House of Commons' (*PS* 81). Here whisky, one of the symbols that Burns was inventing for Scotland, becomes a serious counter in the discussion of the British polity (by contrast, Burns's predecessor in the Scots poetry tradition, Robert Fergusson, tainted the beverage by his habitual association of it with the Highland police-force employed in Edinburgh, whom he deprecated at every turn). The complaint of the poem is against what Burns and others saw as punitive taxes against Scottish distillers, imposed after gin makers in England had protested that their market was being flooded by the cheaper beverage from Scotland (some of this price differential being to do with the unfair advantage enjoyed in the first place by illicit distillation in Scotland). 'The Author's Earnest Cry and Prayer' begins by sardonically addressing 'Ye IRISH LORDS' (l. 1), some of whom had Scottish seats in parliament, and so immediately essays a situation of incongruence in constitutional affairs. There is sly irony also as the narrator entreats the Scottish members to inform about the situation the prime minister, William Pitt, 'yon PREMIER YOUTH' (l. 19), and so again is signalled unbalanced polity. Generally, as the poem considers various Scottish and English politicians, it depicts a complicated, constitutionally unjust Britain in which even the talented statesman cannot begin to effect a coherent plan of government. The rather rambling comedy of the poem becomes changed in mood in the 'Postscript', where a bitter note is sounded as the figure of the highland warrior is drawn upon. After the failure of the 1745 Jacobite rebellion, the highlanders, like other Scots, are now prominent in the service of the British state:

> But bring a SCOTCHMAN frae his hill,
> Clap in his cheek a *highlan gill*,
> Say, such is royal George's will,
>   An' there's the foe,
> He has nae thought but how to kill
>   Twa at a blow.

(ll. 163–8)

The poem ends sententiously, but ambivalently, with the idea that 'FREEDOM and WHISKY gang thegither' (l. 185). With angry hyperbolic implication, the question is posed, will the Scots need to fight the English to have the taxation laws more equitably arranged? Although far from representing a consummate political critique, the poem sees Burns utilizing the Scottish situation to comment thoughtfully upon the difficulty of attaining a cogent British polity. If not exactly a poem of 'Scottish nationalism' it is a text that looks sardonically at the 'British nation'.

A highly scornful perspective upon the British nation is found in 'The Twa Dogs. A Tale' (*PS* 71), a confident choice by Burns with which to begin the Kilmarnock edition. The poem is a very slyly cultured piece. On the one hand it is an animal fable featuring two talking dogs who meet in a highly regionalized space: "'TWAS in that place o' *Scotland*'s isle, / That bears the name o' auld king COIL' (ll. 1–2). However, contradicting this site of blinkered, ignorant focus (Scotland is not an island, and Kyle is not a particularly important place within it that demands cognizance be taken of its historical origins), the text is also a recognizably 'cultured' performance in its polished couplets

47

and in its controlled digressive style, common features of 'mainstream' political and social satire in eighteenth-century poetry. Caesar, the dog of a gentleman, and Luath (named after Cuchullin's dog in Macpherson's *Fingal*), a ploughman's dog (to be identified, then, with Burns in his Ossianic enthusiasm) are at ease with one another in spite of their class difference. Caesar, we are told, is happy meeting any among his species, 'An stroan't [pissed] on stanes an' hillocks wi' him' (l. 22). As Liam McIlvanney has observed, the humour here 'lies in the conceit by which pissing in public becomes an index of a civilized mind, free from narrow prejudice'.[3] The contrast the poem implies is between the false refinement of human society and the greater sympathy in the animal world, where Caesar and Luath are 'thick the gither; / Wi' social *nose* whyles snuff'd an' snowcket [poked about with the nose]' (ll. 38–9). In such intimacy Caesar feels able to question (in a way, by implication, his master does not) the lot of the poor such as Luath lives with. Caesar observes that even the lowly huntsman's assistant eats better than a tenant farmer (such as Burns was, and as his father had been):

> Our *Whipper-in*, wee, blastiet wonner,   [accursed; wonder (ironically)
> Poor, worthless elf, it eats a dinner,
> Better than ony *Tenant-man*

(ll. 65–7)

Here through the eyes of the dog the human servant is seen as a 'worthless' creature nonetheless to be fed regularly, and so a nice inversion is accomplished, which probably registers also some historic bitterness from those of Burns's background towards the supposedly better-off servant class. Luath acknowledges that, indeed, a cotter and his family suffer poor material conditions, though still 'They're maistly wonderfu' contented' (l. 84) and breed clever, strapping offspring, in response to which Caesar is perplexed, since he observes that the gentry regard the common folk with the disdain he would show for 'a stinkan brock [badger]' (l. 92). Here again a nice point is made to tell as Caesar's snobbery is biologically explicable, but humans do not show solidarity within their own species. Luath elaborates that the cotters have their wives and children, 'the dearest comfort o' their lives' (l. 111), and that they are made even more comfortable by a little cheap ale. Securely based in their lives, they are not slow to comment on local church affairs, particularly 'patronage' (l. 119), where local landowners by the eighteenth century increasingly seek to circumvent the traditional rights of the ordinary congregation to appoint their own parish minister, and which so many Presbyterians of the humblest class successfully resisted.

Likewise, these common folk comment on affairs of state, and 'ferlie [wonder] at the folk in LON'ON' (l. 122), their opinions being informed by their reading of newspapers (a matter of implicit pride in the poem is the Presbyterian insistence on literacy for everyone as a means of accessing Scripture). There is a nice reversal as the wonder, or incredulity, in the face of metropolitan mores is balanced by mention of the supposedly primitive or superstitious customs of the common folk of the poem as they celebrate hogmanay. We have here, however, not mere social realism, but Burns building upon the poem's proud observation of Presbyterian common culture (in matters such as independent intellect) as he supplements this with a literary scene imported from Robert Fergusson's 'The Daft-Days' (1772). Specifically, this involves an image in Fergusson's poem of the ordinary folk sheltering indoors at hogmanay in Edinburgh and passing round a common beaker of beer. In 'The Twa Dogs' Burns transposes the scene (so that it becomes less quasi-liturgical in the Episcopalian or even Catholic manner), and instead 'The luntan [puffing] pipe, an' sneeshin mill [snuffbox], / Are handed round wi' right guid will' (ll. 133–4). Yet again, then, in the manner that he employs in 'The Cotter's Saturday Night', Burns is working hard to counter the conception of the rebarbative Presbyterian figure.

As in the case of Mailie the sheep, we find in 'The Twa Dogs' another animal literate in the 'dismal science' of economics. Luath explains that, in contrast to the settled customs of the peasant folk, there is now abroad the disruptive profit motive of the agrarian revolution (where in many areas of Scotland smaller farms are condensed into much larger ones, so as to bring about economies of scale). Not only this, but Luath, appropriately enough for a poet's dog, exercises in his explanation an ironic wit of the kind shown by Alexander Pope (along with Thomson, Ramsay and Fergusson, the poet most alluded to in Burns's work). Probably evident is Burns's reading

of Pope's 'Epistle to Bathurst', lampooning the excesses of the
South Sea Company scandal of the 1720s with a conflation of
natural imagery and punning upon the world of speculation,
when Luath comments on an increasing trend seen in the lives
of small farmers:

> There's monie a creditable *stock*
> O' decent, honest, fawsont folk,   [respectable
> Are riven out baith root an' branch.

(ll. 141–3)

Such a tragedy perhaps happens, speculates Luath, because the
stewards of greater men ruthlessly manage the estates of the
gentry, while the latter are distracted by great affairs of state, or
while engaged 'for Britain's guid' (l. 148). The humble dog
speaks here either in naivety, or, more likely, because he is at
one with the peasantry with whom he lives in seeking to think
well of people as an initial mental reflex. The candid Caesar,
however, corrects such a seemingly reasonable notion and
launches a searing indictment on the new class of country
gentry, as he pictures the aristocratic cadet typically on his
grand tour in Europe. In counterpoint to the peasantry, well
integrated with the nature that they husband, the young
landowner is seen selfishly and noisily at odds with his
environment abroad:

> There, at VIENNA or VERSAILLES,
> He rives his father's auld entails;   [bursts; patrimony
> Or by MADRID he takes the rout,
> To thrum *guittarres* an' fecht wi' *nowt*;   [fight; cattle (often oxen)
> Or down *Italian Vista* startles,
> Wh-re-hunting amang groves o' myrtles:
> Then bowses drumlie *German-water*,   [boozes; dark
> To make himsel look fair an' fatter,
> An' clear the consequential sorrows,
> Love-gifts of Carnival Signorias.
> *For Britain's guid*! for her destruction!
> Wi' dissipation, feud an' faction!

(ll. 159–70)

Assaulting the places they visit, these dilettantes are full of
artifice and disease, an obstreperous state of affairs, implicitly,
that stands them in good stead for the party politics ('feud an'

50

faction') they indulge in when they take their seats in parliament. The functionless lives of the ruling classes (those who presume to be the natural political functionaries) are further painted by Caesar in a way that contrasts with the already described healthy (though increasingly assaulted) lives of the peasantry. And this fractured, topsy-turvy world is commented upon with facetious but also bitter comedy as the dogs go their separate ways, resolving to meet again soon, but rejoicing 'they were na *men* but *dogs*' (l. 236).

In 'The Twa Dogs' Burns is incredulous of the conceit of the well-working, country-wealth-based British polity. In another poem from the Kilmarnock edition, 'A Dream' (*PS* 113), he is iconoclastic again in the face of the powers that be. This poem is inspired by Burns's reading in a newspaper of Thomas Warton's Pindaric 'Ode XVII for His Majesty's Birthday, June 4th 1786'. In his work Warton says that George III deserves a number of 'bards' to celebrate the sovereign's great wisdom and justice. Burns, intent at this period of his life in constructing his 'bardic' role, obviously felt the pull of an 'invitation' to which he should respond. Burns's response, however, offers not praise but a survey of all that is falling apart under George's rule. Pointedly, in the 'Christ's Kirk' stanza, associated with the cultured Stuart kings of Scotland, Burns turns the Scots language into a venomous weapon:

> I see ye're complimented thrang,   [earnestly
>   By many a *lord* an' *lady*;
> 'God save the King' 's a cukoo sang
>   That's unco easy said ay:
> The *Poets* too, a venal gang,
>   Wi' rhymes weel-turn'd an' ready,
> Wad gar you trow ye ne'er do wrang,   [believe
>   But ay unerring steady,
>   On sic a day.

(ll. 10–18)

Among George's mismanagement are the loss of the American colonies, higher taxation and his siring of a dissolute son, the Prince of Wales. It is interesting that Burns, rather careful about what he included in the Kilmarnock edition, here feels no need to temper, if not treasonable, at least cynical expression towards the royal dynasty. Mrs Dunlop suggested to the poet that this

piece if included in future editions of his work might harm his
sales, especially in London, but Burns responded that expun-
ging or excising this work in any way was not up for
negotiation. Hugh Blair, in commenting on the poem in advance
of the publication of the Edinburgh edition, censured only lines
in the poem that crudely depict the lust of another of the royal
offspring, Prince William, but does not quibble with the
sentiments, in general, in the text. What all this tells us is that
the age of 'politeness' into which Burns's published work was
undoubtedly launched was not one that was necessarily
politically conservative (an equation that has sometimes been
all too readily made by Burns criticism).

One of the most celebrated poems in the Kilmarnock edition
is the obliquely political piece 'To a Mouse, On Turning Her up
in Her Nest, with the Plough, November, 1785' (*PS* 69). This
poem highlights well the tension between the 'heaven-taught
ploughman' and Burns the literary artist. A staple of Burns lore
is the poet's brother Gilbert's account of Burns composing the
poem with plough in hand. There may well be an element of
truth here, but this emphasis tends towards underestimating a
thoughtfully allusive performance that suggests substantial
revisionary polish was applied to the poem. A thread that runs
throughout the text is the projection of human values onto the
animal the narrator encounters. Thus he refers to the perception
of the mouse that the narrator is intent on 'murd'ring' (l. 6) her,
and the idea that the creature knows how to 'thieve' (l. 13).
There is a twist to this anthropomorphism, however, delivered
in stanza two:

> I'm truly sorry Man's dominion
> Has broken Nature's social union,
> An' justifies that ill opinion,
>> Which makes thee startle,
> At me, thy poor, earth-born companion,
>> An' *fellow mortal*!

(ll. 7–12)

As in 'The Twa Dogs', there is something sinister about mankind
as it is nature, paradoxically, that is more truly 'social' than
humanity. The apprehension in the text here looks towards the
pessimism inherent in the Romantic attitude in opposition to

the progressive optimism of the late eighteenth century. The ruination of the dumb creature's habitation ought to be read against Burns's own experiences of seeing his father's travails at Lochlea farm, which the family came close to losing during 1783–4, when sued by their landlord over rent arrears. At a time when landowners were realizing spiralling rents from smaller farmers, William Burnes agreed to pay a very high fee for land that was extremely marshy and, according to Burns himself, both the work on this unyielding terrain and the stress of attempting to meet his payments on it contributed to his father's demise. The mouse in Burns's poem wants very little, receives very little and is now wantonly chastised:

> That wee-bit heap o' leaves an' stibble,
> Has cost thee monie a weary nibble!
> Now thou's turn'd out, for a' thy trouble.
>
> (ll. 31–3)

The apprehension throughout 'To a Mouse' is close to the perception sometimes of James Thomson in *The Seasons* of man's domineering attitude to nature and to animals; even worse, Burns's text implies, is the cruelty of the world under human direction to man:

> But Mousie, thou art no thy-lane,   [thy-self
> In proving *foresight* may be vain:
> The best laid schemes o' *Mice* an' *Men*,
>   Gang aft agley,   [awry
> An' lea'e us nought but grief an' pain,
>   For promis'd joy!
>
> (ll. 37–42)

The small man often struggles beneath forces much bigger than he himself can realistically control, an apprehension appropriate to an age of increasing bankruptcy and uncertainty within the circumstances of speculative agriculture and economics generally. 'To a Mouse' ends with the idea of particular human uncertainty that separates man from nature:

> Still, thou art blest, compar'd wi' *me*!
> The *present* only toucheth thee:
> But Och! I *backward* cast my e'e,
>   On prospects drear!
> An' *forward*, tho' I canna *see*,

53

I *guess* an' *fear*!

(ll. 43–8)

This stanza, a transposition to some extent of a passage in Johnson's *Rasselas*, paints the human mind deeply unsettled. The poem, then, has arched from identification with a very humble animal appropriate to the age of sensibility (and can we really believe that Burns as a working farmer would be prone when literally at the plough to pay much regard to a creature that could be a pest, so far as his livelihood was concerned?) towards a dark literary dissociation from nature that shows Burns in the vanguard of the coming Romantic movement.

In the Edinburgh edition Burns introduces 'A Fragment: When Guilford Good Our Pilot Stood' (*PS* 38) on the American situation, a poem that he wrote possibly in 1784. Burns thought of including this political ballad in the Kilmarnock edition but decided not to, and yet, as we see in 'A Dream', from the beginning Burns was not averse to critiquing British politics. A clue to the omission lies perhaps in the remark made by Hugh Blair, according to John Gibson Lockhart, in response to 'When Guilford Good' that Burns's politics 'smell of the smithy'. Sometimes interpreted as pointing to an apprehension of Burns's 'left-wing' politics, the identification is more credibly interpreted as an iconoclasm, generally, on Burns's part with regard to politics and politicians, and this is precisely what 'When Guilford Good' provides. Burns omits the poem, possibly, because it displays a cynicism too riotously comprehensive to be in keeping with the innocent bardic image he was minting in his first book. Guilford, Lord North, an important minister throughout the prosecution of the American war, is represented handling the rudder of the boat, the ship of state, only for the scene immediately to shift, in farcical manoeuvre, to that of the Boston tea party. In this squib, Charles Fox and other prominent figures of the government in London are also ridiculed, while celebrated is Richard Montgomery, an officer in Washington's army and a man Burns associates with one of the martial Ayrshire families he eulogizes in 'The Vision'. Vicariously, though not entirely to be taken seriously, the ancient enmity between Scotland and England is extended into North America. The swirling, chaotic scenario of the piece is confirmed by references towards the end of the poem to the accompaniment of the bagpipes as the British go into action against the Americans. Not really a critique of 'imperialism' as such, the poem simply satirizes much directionless and incoherent activity on the part of the British state (the pun on Guilford and ironically exploded 'guile' is a key to the scathing knockabout humour of the text).

Ten years after 'When Guilford Good', Burns is armed with the political vocabulary of the French Revolution to comment more cogently on American independence in 'Ode [For General Washington's Birthday]' (*PS* 451). Burns sent a draft of the text to Mrs Dunlop on 25 June 1794, enthusiastically declaiming to her, 'The Subject is, LIBERTY: you know, my honored Friend, how dear the theme is to me' (*L* ii. 297), but she retorted in a letter that his theme was these days, following the period of terror in France, associated with butchery; the breach between the pair widened from this point, with Dunlop ignoring letters from the poet and only resuming their correspondence as he lay on his deathbed in the summer of 1796. Around this time also, Burns, in the employ of the crown, found himself increasingly under a little political suspicion, and the 'Ode' was not published in his lifetime, and, indeed, not until 1872, a fact that shows the long nineteenth-century nervousness over literature in Britain that sided with the revolutionary ideals of the late eighteenth century. In attempting in the text a Pindaric ode, an irregular form (though peddling, as Matthew Arnold famously said, an 'intoxication in style'), Burns harks back to Milton (though he was familiar with the form from the work of Dryden also). Metrically Burns's performance is not quite up to his usual sure-footed performance, but it is rousing in its rhetoric as it hymns Washington's America and its constitution:

> But come, ye sons of Liberty,
> Columbia's offspring, brave as free,
> In danger's hour still flaming in the van:
> Ye know, and dare maintain, The Royalty of Man.

> (ll. 25–8)

Though this is not explicitly about the French deposition of royalty, nonetheless the vocabulary of the revolutionary 1790s rather than the 1770s is clear. The poem posits the ancient principle of the 'freeborn Briton' (l. 32), found in the case of England in the wise kingship of Alfred and in Scotland with William Wallace (an appearance that perhaps explains Burns's hope for a better reception for the piece from Mrs Dunlop, Wallace's descendant). Burns, then, reveals himself again in an interesting British literary and cultural context that was, for instance, finding at this time new uses for the 'republican' Milton and locating in ancient British history, such as the Anglo-Saxon period and the Magna Carta, a tradition of liberty that was constructed by a broad grouping of radicals and dissenters currently under the cosh in Britain. As in the contemporaneous 'Robert Bruce's March to Bannockburn', we see Burns broadening (for himself, at least) the iconic base of this 'British' tradition with Wallace, in a manoeuvre that it is helpful to see in tandem also with his celebration of the seventeenth-century Covenanters, likewise brought in from the cold at this time by some political thinkers as proponents of 'liberty'. In the context of the explicit subject matter of Burns's ode, the 'liberty' written into the American constitution resulted from a document among whose architects were Scots-descended individuals whose sense of democracy was deeply informed by a potent combination of Enlightenment social contractarianism and the Presbyterian insistence on individual conscience. Burns's 'Ode', then, is a work that represents one of Burns's most-wide ranging essays on politics.

Another trenchant political poem not published until after Burns's death, this time in 1818, though written in 1786, is 'Address of Beelzebub' (PS 108), where Burns again sees America as the ground on which freedom most certainly stands. One of Burns's most savagely satirical poems, it sees the devil hailing John, Earl of Breadalbane, for helping prevent emigration from the Highlands by natives struggling for subsistence, whom landlords feared would bring about a shortage of labour should they depart for America and Canada (a very strikingly ironic moment in Scottish history, given the later clearances of the nineteenth century when highlanders were forcibly driven from the land by landlords to make way for more profitable sheep). Burns makes sardonic capital from the 'fighting Jock' myth as the devil says that if the would-be emigrants were to succeed in their plan they might in North America be led by some fearless leader (the iconic Ayrshire name of Montgomery is again numbered among such) as is to be found there, 'Till, God knows what may be effected' (l. 17). The devil splutters:

> what right hae they
> To Meat, or Sleep, or light o' day,
> Far less to riches, pow'r, or freedom,
> But what your lordships PLEASE TO GIE THEM?

(ll. 27–30)

This is a remarkable moment in Lowland Scottish literature, as Burns speaks out on behalf of injustice towards the Gael, when previously Anglophone Scottish writers displayed a long hostility to the Highlands, or at best during the eighteenth century (as in the Ossianic productions of Macpherson) swathed the Gaidheal-tachd in empty, socially unrealistic romance. Burns's Beelzebub encompasses the entire range of racist insult practised so often in Britain upon the Scottish highlanders, such as their dumb insolence, or 'Highlan spirit' (l. 38); their drunken idleness: 'Let WARK an' HUNGER mak them sober!' (l. 42); and their promiscuity: 'Wi a' their bastarts on their back!' (l. 52). He also recommends putting young Highland girls to work in Drury Lane as prostitutes so that they might be of some service, and beating the highlanders generally with the best and longest whips available. The highlander was a bogeyman in the British mentality for much of the eighteenth century, and, remarkably, Burns here begins to counter the stereotype, finding individuals more victimized than fearsome. Breadalbane was President of the Highland Society which met in Covent Garden, overseeing the economy and culture of the Highlands. Burns, then, even as implicitly he extends the Enlightenment concept of human 'sympathy' to the highlanders (erroneously rendered as animals in the mentality of Breadalbane and his colleagues), opposes another strand of Enlightenment thinking in its regulatory schemes of 'improvement'. Beelzebub ends by promising Breadalbane a cosy fireside niche in hell, near to Herod and the likes of Pizarro, conqueror of Peru (a nice touch, in that a strong conception among the British polity was that it encompassed individuals very different from those of such despotic activities as might be associated with Catholic Spain). With 'Address of Beelzebub' we have a text that Burns seems never to have

57

thought possible for publication in either the Kilmarnock or the Edinburgh editions, and an example from the poet's wide reserved canon of political, religious and bawdy pieces that remained only obscurely known in Burns's own lifetime.

It is true that Burns to some extent practised self-censorship and that others (from Hugh Blair to Mrs Dunlop, who was not keen on showing to others the letter in which Burns had drafted parts of his ode for Washington) joined in this process. We should be careful, however, as some Burns criticism has not been, about suggesting a deep conspiracy to silence Burns, as though the future of the British polity hung upon the potency of his words. Vague claims have been made, including by Hugh MacDiarmid, about scholars being blocked in their attempts to gain access to information about Burns's true political affiliations. The implication is that Burns was a deeply subversive 'radical' who had to hide his views for fear of prosecution. Burns, in fact, was if anything too unguarded in his comments, writing with enthusiasm to a disapproving Mrs Dunlop of his approval of the execution of the French royal family. He also reported to Mrs Dunlop on 2 January 1793 that 'some envious, malicious devil has raised a little demur on my political principles' (L ii. 170) – and promised that henceforth he would be much more guarded about his views.

What Burns feared, though, was not so much being dragged off to prison, but losing out on advancement in the excise service over his views, not quite the same thing as dealing in and worrying over treason. On being promoted to acting supervisor in the excise, he wrote with elation to Mrs Dunlop on 29 December 1794, 'My Political sins seem to be forgiven me' (L ii. 333), and the whole set of circumstances suggests that Burns was never under very serious government suspicion. There is also the matter of the *Rosamond*, when Burns was party to the seizure of this smuggling vessel in February 1792 from the contraband of which the poet supposedly paid for and despatched carronades, or large guns, for service among the pro-revolutionaries of France. At this time, however, Britain was not at war with France, and Burns felt no conflict of interest and none, if the story is true (some scholars believe the story of the carronades to be merely a romantic invention of the Tory John Gibson Lockhart), was imputed to him by his superiors.

58

Another item in the lore of Burns's political principles is the poet's membership of the Dumfries Volunteers, a militia loyal to the government and formed, as others were up and down the country, as Britain, now at war with revolutionary France, feared invasion. Along with John Syme (a fellow crown employee) and William Maxwell (Burns's physician, who had supposedly been enthusiastically present at the execution of King Louis XVI), Burns applied to join his local militia in January 1795. Extreme theories about Burns's motivations have abounded, ranging from his acting out of fear over his suspected political loyalties to his sheer self-interest, seeing the Volunteers as a means of winning respectability for himself and adding to the chances of promotion within his profession. Certainly, Burns had been vocal, including in his poetry, in satirizing the Loyal Natives Club of Dumfries, a pompous drinking club formed in the town in 1793 which was bound together by members' hatred of revolutionary France and their expressions of unswerving loyalty to the government. The most certain testimony of the time is Burns's song 'The Dumfries Volunteers' (*PS* 484), which, with its opening line of 'Does haughty Gaul invasion threat', is sometimes taken to be akin to Coleridge's 'Fears in Solitude' in representing a recantation of revolutionary fervour in the face of a very real prospect of foreign invasion. The text denies that any 'foreign tinkler-loun [fellow]' (l. 19) should interfere with the British political situation, though it acknowledges also that abuses most certainly do exist in Britain. Ultimately, it consists of a rather artificial appeal to unity: 'O, let us not, like snarling tykes, / In wrangling be divided' (ll. 9–10), and 'while we sing, GOD SAVE THE KING, / We'll ne'er forget THE PEOPLE!' (ll. 31–2). It is an uncertain text that sees Burns sincerely attempting to juggle understandable fears about the designs of a foreign power and his own pro-revolutionary principles to which the last word ('the people') is given.

In so far as Burns's 'party politics' can be pinned down, it is certainly the case that his sentiments in favour of the American and French revolutions show him to be a 'Whig', a term he embraces in several places. For instance, in 'A Fragment – On Glenriddel's Fox Breaking His Chain' (*PS* 527) the poet celebrates the escape of his friend's pet fox as:

> a Whig without a stain,
> A Whig in principle and grain,
> Couldst thou enslave a free-born creature,
> A native denizen of Nature?

(ll. 17–20)

Burns's Whiggishness also extends to taking the part of the Jamaican slave in a song he perhaps wrote or perhaps simply collected, 'The Slave's Lament', but this solitary item serves only to highlight how little interest he took in the pro-abolitionist cause, unlike many other Whigs of radical bent during the period, such as the editor of his first collected poems, James Currie, or the English writer he admired, William Roscoe (and we might remember also that Burns had contemplated becoming a manager on a plantation, though this is not to argue that he is not entitled to change his mind).

The politics of the day feature in his rather overblown, melodramatic 'Ode to the Departed Regency-bill – 1789' completed in March of 1789. Responding to uncertainty over the king's madness and the various parliamentary manoeuvrings surrounding this, Burns is scathing of both sides, Tory and Whig. Infamously, he wrote of this piece to Mrs Dunlop, 'I have this moment finished the following political Squib ... Politics is dangerous ground for me to tread on, and yet I cannot for the soul of me resist an impulse of any thing like Wit' (*L* i. 392). Burns is saying that politics are grist to his 'Wit' or imagination, rather than of primary importance to him; which is not to say that politics are unimportant to him, merely that he is no ideologue at the cost of all else. In 1790, at precisely the time when Burns is constructing his Whig identity, he is still capable of writing sentimental Jacobite songs (a tendency which, alongside his bardic persona, had allowed many acquaintances to see him as essentially a Tory). In this year he writes 'Awa Whigs Awa', which, even allowing for the slightly different usage of 'Whig' in the Scottish historical context, is rather odd if Burns is serious about taking active part in the increasingly ideologically riven 1790s between 'Tory' and 'Whig'. In '[The Heron Ballads]' of 1795, Burns involves himself in supporting Patrick Heron, the 'Whig' candidate for the Stewartry of Kirkcudbright. As the research of Norman R. Paton has shown, however, Heron operated under a nominal label, being no supporter of Charles Fox, the Whig leader in Britain, and was backed by Henry Dundas, the closest ally in Scotland of the Tory prime minister, William Pitt.[4] At the very best, then, Burns in his support for Heron was naively innocent, but it is unlikely that he would be unaware of his candidate's actual connections. Burns's 'true' politics remain a vexed area to the present day, but what seems less uncertain is his emotional involvement, generally, on the side of liberal causes during the 1790s.

5

Women, Love and the Body

The most certain area of Robert Burns's personal notoriety concerns sex. The poet sired at least thirteen children to at least five women and had a series of affairs and liaisons, the precise number of which is not easily computed by biographers. The weighing of Burns's machismo, however, should not be allowed to obscure the nuances of his writings about women, sex and the body, some of which, at least, have to do with the cultural and intellectual climate in which Burns existed and to which he sought to respond.

'A Poet's Welcome to his love-begotten Daughter; the first instance that entitled him to the venerable appellation of Father' (*PS* 60) sees Burns in emotional and combative mood. He peddles a powerful mixture of love for his first child – his illegitimate daughter born on 22 May 1785 to Elizabeth Paton, his mother's serving-girl – and a defiant savouring of the label 'Fornicator', that category of sinner loudly proclaimed by the kirk with its public chastisement of offenders upon the 'cutty-stool'. The poem has Burns in an attitude that is best summed up as pro-life:

> THOU's welcome, Wean! Mischanter fa' me, [misfortune
> If thoughts o' thee, or yet thy Mamie,
> Shall ever daunton me or awe me,
>   My bonie lady;
> Or if I blush when thou shalt ca' me
>   Tyta, or Daddie.

(ll. 1–6)

The real sin would be denial of the existence and validity (which orthodox Christian morality would frown upon) of this daughter, and, indeed, of the feelings between the parents that

62

have produced the child. In one of his characteristic hallmarks as a poet, Burns subversively inhabits the language of religion and utters a prayer for a daughter who is 'love-begotten' (a reversal of a phrase in common parlance, 'ill-begotten'):

> Lord grant that thou may ay inherit
> Thy Mither's looks an' gracefu' merit;
> An' thy poor, worthless Daddie's spirit,
>> Without his failins!
> 'Twad please me mair to see thee heir it
>> Than stocked mailins!   [farmsteads
>
> (ll. 37–42)

Here Burns seizes the moral high-ground, appropriating the deepest tenets of the age of sensibility, its promotion of the primacy of a good-oriented 'natural man' and of the inner, benevolent feelings as social cement *a priori* to the institutional endorsement of human relationships. Written contemporaneously in 1785 with the foregoing poem, 'The Fornicator. A New Song' (*PS* 61), swaggeringly rejoices in the revelation 'before the [Kirk] Congregation wide' (l. 9) that the narrator is 'a proven Fornicator' (l. 8). The lover refuses to be cowed, joyously recounting that as he and his Betsey sit at the front of the church in a position of public excoriation, his

> downcast eye by chance did spy
> ....
> Those limbs so clean where I, between,
> Commenc'd a Fornicator.
>
> (ll. 13 and 15–16)

What does he have to repent since, unlike some who consort with prostitutes, his lover and he have made a free exchange untainted by money or disease out of pure attraction? Calculated to offend the Presbyterian moral atmosphere of his locality, Burns's poem sees him rejoice in the persona of frank, healthy and clubbable young hot-blooded male:

> Ye wenching blades whose hireling jades
>> Have tipt you off blue-boram,   [have passed on the pox
> I tell ye plain, I do disdain
>> To rank you in the Quorum;
> But a bony lass upon the grass
>> To teach her esse Mater,

And no reward but for regard,
  O that's a Fornicator.

(ll. 33-40)

Burns the libertine fully emerges in 'Libel Summons' (1786; *PS* 109), a work, like the previous two pieces discussed, not published during the poet's lifetime. Whether or not Burns actually formed the 'Court of Equity' described in the poem to sit in judgement upon their fellow 'Fornicators by profession' (l. 5) has been debated, but given the comic exaggeration of the poem the text itself can be taken as evidence of very little except Burns enjoying the idea of a regulatory association of rakes operating in parallel to the court of the kirk session (the job of which was to consider and publicly investigate instances of immorality among Presbyterian parishioners). The first section of the poem prescribes the remit of the Court of Equity to summon and judge those who disown the female they have ruined, those who indulge merely in heavy petting, those who practise *coitus interruptus* and those who turn down the sexual overtures of a woman. The 'ideal' of a thoughtlessly honest and brave 'fornicator', then, is circumscribed. Thereafter, the officials of the court are assembled:

> FIRST, POET B—s he takes the chair,
> Allow'd by a', his title's fair;
> And pass'd nem. con. without dissension,
> He has a Duplicate pretension.

(ll. 29-32)

Here Burns acknowledges that by now Jean Armour, as well as Elizabeth Paton, has borne him a child out of wedlock. The poem more widely, however, might be described as revealing the 'duplicate pretension' of the world, where sexual congress is on the minds of most individuals, albeit secretly, as much as their everyday business. We have such an instance when a summons to judgement is read before the court for John Brown the clockmaker, for denying 'outright' what he has been up to with a young woman. As he is accused, Brown's hypocrisy is stripped away in a searing innuendo that appropriates the description of his profession:

> That ye hae bred a hurly-burly
> 'Bout JEANY MITCHEL's tirlie-whirlie,   [pudendum muliebre

64

And blooster'd at her regulator,
Till a' her wheels gang clitter-clatter.

(ll. 63–6)

Brown is further charged with attempting to administer poison
to Jenny's unborn child, and even though this charge is couched
in ridiculously comical terms as 'a tale [that] might even in hell
be scandal!' (l. 68), the hyperbole is not without serious point:
humanity will stoop to anything to maintain appearances of
moral, upright citizenship. Toward the end of the poem the
punishment to which another hypocrite is sentenced, displayed
naked at the town centre with his penis tightly bound, both
parodies the public humiliation of the cutty-stool and implies its
actually voyeuristic and even sadomasochistic function for the
supposedly pure-of-heart moralists of the kirk:

> Our beadles to the Cross shall take you,
> And there shall mither naked make you;
> Some canie grip near by your middle,   [skilful
> They shall it bind as tight's a fiddle.

(ll. 141–4)

At the heart of many of Burns's poems and songs dealing with
human sexuality is an identification of the hypocrisy of society.
Published three years after Burns's death, *The Merry Muses of
Caledonia* (1799) was a collection of bawdy songs probably
compiled by Burns in 1792. This material was sometimes written
by Burns, sometimes merely gathered by him for the use of the
Crochallan Fencibles, a drinking club whose title parodied the
idea of a civil militia and which met in Daniel Douglas's tavern in
Edinburgh. The collection opens with a version of 'The
Fornicator', before going on to express both the joyous exertions
of the body and a satirical view of institutions that would stand in
the way of free sexual expression. One piece, 'Errock Brae' (*MM*
11), not originally by Burns, reveals the robust Scottish tradition
of anti-Calvinist satire, a context upon which he drew for the likes
of 'Holy Willie's Prayer'. Its final stanza mocks each of the three
main denominations of eighteenth-century Scotland:

> A Prelate he loups on before,   [leaps
>   A Catholic behin',
> But gie me a Cameronian,   [Calvinist
>   He'll m-w a body blin'.   [mow, mowe (copulate)

65

We encounter also the original bawdy version of 'Comin Thro' the Rye' (*MM* 39) that Burns transformed on a different occasion so that it became a respectable staple of the folk-pastoral canon of Scotland. The pawkiness of the original version harmonizes exactly with Burns's observation elsewhere of human hypocrisy over sex:

> Mony a body meets a body,
> They dare na weel avow;
> Mony a body f—s a body,
> Ye wad na think it true.

Two pieces, both substantially Burns's work, stand out in the volume. The first of these is the song beginning 'Yestreen I Had a Pint o' Wine' (*PS* 320), of which Burns, writing to George Thomson in 1793, proclaimed the belief that it was 'the best love-song I ever composed in my life; but in its *original* state, is not quite a lady's song' (*L* ii. 206). The version published by Thomson, probably closely directed by Burns, politely generalized the rapture that is so explicitly orgasmic in the first version found in *The Merry Muses* (*MM* 9). The earlier version also contained two stanzas, allegedly a 'Postscript by Another Hand' that, if not by Burns, ventriloquize his inner attitude with striking accord. The tenor of these stanzas leads one to the speculation that Burns in fact wrote these lines and that his disavowal was a clever device for couching the notion that his heterodox attitude could find a chime in others. As with the rest of the composition these stanzas defiantly proclaim a tender and physical love for Anne Park, the fifth woman we are certain of to become pregnant by Burns. She was a teenage barmaid with whom the poet enjoyed trysts at the Globe Tavern in Dumfries, probably fully known about by Burns's wife, Jean. Reading the lines of the 'Postscript' biographically, then, we reach a perhaps disturbing awareness of Burns's flaunting of the institution of marriage, but there is a passionate disregard for other institutions that is also compelling:

> The kirk and state may join and tell;
> To do sic things I manna:
> The kirk and state may gae to h—ll,
> An' I shall gae to Anna.

The finest piece in *The Merry Muses* is Burns's 'Poor Bodies Do Naething But M-w' (*MM* 80), that responds specifically to Edmund Burke's jibe in 1790 against the common people of Britain, whom he feared might be inspired by the events of the French Revolution, that they were the 'swinish multitude'. If the people are dumb animals, this song retorts, then why should they not spend their time in copulation? Alongside such innocent bestial activity is counterpointed the feverish war-mongering undertaken by those superiors of the people, the royalty of Europe. This frank, rollicking satire encompassing comment on the contemporary politics of Britain, France, Germany and Poland shows yet again that even within Burns's reserved canon of work, here bawdy pieces collected for his intimate drinking cronies, the poet's licentiousness is not an end in itself but forms part of a critique of the true moral difficulties thrown up by the world.

Burns's sympathetic treatment of the body, and the female body in particular, is found in his early published work in subtle, differently 'reserved' form in one of the showpieces of the Kilmarnock edition, 'To a Louse, on Seeing One on a Lady's Bonnet at Church' (*PS* 83), written, probably, toward the end of 1785. It is a poem where Burns observes the natural condition of humanity while displaying an affectionately realistic portrait of a young woman in a compromised position that she does not realize for herself. It is an occasional comical piece but deals also with the profound issue of human perception. As the male gaze falls upon the pretty Jenny in her Sunday best, it observes upon her hair the parasitic louse. The narrator verbally chastises the insect for its presumption:

> Ye ugly, creepan, blastet wonner,
> Detested, shunn'd, by saunt an' sinner,
> How daur ye set your fit upon her,   [foot
> Sae fine a *Lady*!

(ll. 7–10)

We are made aware, then, that this creature is the lowliest possible, detested both by good and bad alike. This identification, however, sees the narrator state the obvious since a dumb animal will, of course, stand outwith the human categories of morality (of 'saint' and 'sinner') and be beyond their construction. The louse is oblivious also to social decorum, prompting the indignant narrator to opine that it would better inhabit a beggar's head. However, in a change of tack, the insect is then seen by the spluttering narrator as an arrogant social climber as the creature will not be satisfied until it has achieved 'the vera tapmost, towrin height / O' *Miss's bonnet*' (ll. 23–4). Encoded within the confused outrage of the narrator is the true concern of the poem: the way in which humans believe themselves to stand apart from nature, and, indeed, throw a cordon sanitaire around their condition, cloaking themselves both with their clothes and with the notion of a hierarchical society. Nature, in actuality, does not respect the special nature of humanity, which is a peculiar conceit of the human mind.

'To a Louse' is a psychological vignette, as Jenny is aware (she thinks) of the male admiration she is attracting but which is a different kind of gaze altogether – 'O *Jenny* dinna toss your head, / An' set your beauties a' abroad [abroad]!' (ll. 37–8).We are led, then, from stupid outrage to comic whimsicality and finally to philosophical musing:

> O wad some Pow'r the giftie gie us
> *To see oursels as others see us!*
> It wad frae monie a blunder free us
> An' foolish notion:
> What airs in dress an' gait wad lea'e us,
> And ev'n Devotion!
>
> (ll. 43–8)

Here we find the idea of 'sympathy' as expounded by Adam Smith in his *Theory of Moral Sentiments* (1759), one of Burns's favourite books. Putting ourselves in place of each other is the mechanism of sympathy; here, though, there is a twist, as we are to imagine ourselves in place of another but looking back at our original self. Although such insight might 'frae monie a blunder free us' (for instance, thinking we are admired when we are not), implicitly we are to be aware that such insight would not be an unalloyed benefit. We would be stripped of our pride, our attitudes, as well as our misapprehensions, even to the extent of losing self-love ('Devotion'). This represents a highly poised ending as, even while the poem recognizes human conceit, the thought is harboured that the world would be a less attractive place without Jenny in her deportment as local belle. There is also, however, a shudder in the poem as the actual continuance between the human and the natural worlds is sighted. And, given the setting of the church, that final word, 'Devotion', points us also to the idea that we might even with fuller perception give up worshipping the God who supposedly tells us that we are separate from and are masters of nature.

Man's admiration for women is celebrated by Burns in his first version of 'Green Grow the Rashes' (*PS* 45), written probably during 1784, and according to the poet representing 'the genuine language of my heart'.[1] The familiar Burnsian theme of the hardship of life is offset by the distaff sex: 'What signifies the life o' man, / An' 'twere na for the lasses, O' (ll. 3–4). The poet speaks as a vehement worshipper of nature and the age of sentiment:

> For you sae douse, ye sneer at this,   [prudent
>   Ye're nought but senseless asses, O:
> The wisest Man the warl' saw,
>   He dearly lov'd the lasses, O.

(ll. 13–16)

The final stanza ends with a flourish as the poet takes the received notion of woman created after man, but has a particularly emphasized feminine nature in control of the situation: 'Her prentice han' she try'd on man, / An' then she made the lasses, O' (ll. 19–20).

The clever, witty and heartfelt piece that is Burns's best-known version of 'Green Grow the Rashes' can be contrasted with other versions of the song that he prepared for publication. It is unclear the extent to which Burns was drawing precisely on a bawdy piece from the folk tradition of Ayrshire, but the two versions of the song collected in *The Merry Muses* show that Burns was in receipt of something earlier of this kind. One version, where a favourite Burnsian theme of church hypocrisy features, suggests the bard's hand deploying crude humour:

> An' ken ye Leezie Lundie, O,
>   The godly Leezie Lundie, O,
> She m—s like reek thro' a' the week,   [mows; steam
>   But finger f—s on Sunday, O.

(MM 29)

The shifts between the bawdy and the folk-pastoral forms that Burns transacts in 'Green Grow the Rashes' are caught in mid-flow in one 'Song' (*PS* 46) written by Burns while he was involved with Elizabeth Paton. This piece shows him poised between conventionally polite, courting sentiment, and sexual exuberance, in a manner that is suggestive of Burns's own psychology then in his awareness of being at that time of life when a respectable tenant farmer ought to make a good match, and of his problematic appetite for a woman from a lower class than his own. To begin with we see the beloved with 'Her hair well buckl'd, her stays well lac'd' (l. 8), but by the end of the piece we have celebration of the author's more intimate desires: 'For her a, b, e, d, and her c, u, n, t, / And Oh, for the joys of a long winter night!!!' (ll. 10–11).

The concerns of social class and love intermingle again in 'Love and Liberty – A Cantata' (*PS* 84), which concerns the mores of vagabonds. 'Love and Liberty' (often referred to as 'The Jolly Beggars') was enjoyed by several of Burns's close friends in private, including Lady Don, the sister of the poet's patron the Earl of Glencairn. Burns made a fair copy of the piece for Lady Don in 1787 and this feminine reception points us towards Burns's liberal attitude to the frank discussion of sexuality by both the sexes, at least amongst the intelligentsia. 'Love and Liberty' was not published during the poet's lifetime however, appearing in chapbook form in 1799 and for the first time in an edition of Burns's work in 1801 by Thomas Duncan, a Glasgow publisher who made something of a speciality in printing 'unauthorized' works by the poet. It is, then, another piece to be marked out as belonging to Burns's reserved canon. The cantata sees a group of tramps gather at Poosie-Nansie's inn, whose landlady's name is glossed by Burns in his note to the piece as 'The Hostess of a noted Caravansary in Mauchline, well known to and much frequented by the lowest orders of Travellers and Pilgrims'. Here we find an Enlightenment anthropological voice lending dignity to the life that is being introduced sheltering from the winter weather:

> First, niest the fire, in auld, red rags,   [next
> Ane sat; weel brac'd wi' mealy bags,
>   And knapsack a' in order;
> His doxy lay within his arm;   [beggar's wench

Wi' USQEBAE an' blankets warm,   [whisky
    She blinket on her Sodger: [soldier
An' ay he gies the tozie drab   [tipsy female
    The tither skelpan kiss,
While she set up her greedy gab,   [mouth
    Just like an aumous dish: [begging bowl
        Ilk smack still, did crack still,
        Just like a cadger's whip;   [travelling hawker
    Then staggering, an' swaggering,
    He roar'd this ditty up.

(ll. 15–28)

Depicted is a very integrated scene where the social harmony that the protagonists have created in their shelter is complemented by the closely worked metaphors where the vagabond woman puts up her mouth to receive from her inamorato, a former soldier, a love token as though begging for alms, and where his song is like the whip applied by the peddler on his cart while travelling the country. The effect is closely realistic and one that refuses to idealize, even while, at the same time, the joyful nature of this human life is admired and the overall effect is what James Kinsley has called 'true pastoral'.[2] In the cantata the woman sings a song telling of how she first fell in love with her soldier, but that soon after she has an affair with the regimental chaplain which is dangerous to both: 'He ventur'd the SOUL, and I risked the BODY' (l. 67). This is a line consonant with 'Love and Liberty' throughout. The pains of the body suffered by the 'gangrel bodies', most obviously in their outdoor lives, are sites of heroic adventure and human hardship as much as any spiritual travail here on earth. The woman is honest and morally licentious, a kind of Moll Flanders devoid of ironic circumscription, representing a character very similar to that celebrated by Burns in the libertarian male form. A second woman sings a song of love to her dead love, 'John Highlandman', a bogey-man figure in British culture (for Lowland Scotland as elsewhere for much of the eighteenth century). The itinerant life of the couple had been idyllic: 'We ranged a' from Tweed to Spey, / An' liv'd like lords an' ladies gay' (ll. 101–2). The social mobility usually denied to the peasantry in this century is here taken up by an even lower class, vagrants, and by a Highland individual stereotypically

71

seen as savage. The woman's song in Lowland Scots celebrates a love that to contemporary eyes would be shockingly almost inter-racial. The highlander is first of all 'banish'd' (l. 105), either legally or euphemistically – he is, perhaps, simply 'on the run' not from some treasonable offence but rather a 'petty' criminal felony – imprisoned at some point and eventually hanged. The woman, however, does not tell us why he is punished. Is he a common criminal? Is he a Jacobite? We do not have enough information to judge, and the woman in her spare narrative simply and obliquely suggests that it is natural that her lover should be pursued in the manner that he is by a culture that merely hates him for his own sake. Yet again, then, we have a voice that is devoid of moral cause and effect (this time with regard to the state) and which tells sparely of the prodigious love and hate that have circumscribed the woman's life.

As the party proceeds, various individuals pair off, and the fiddler, having lost out on one object of desire, finds success with another:

> But hurchin Cupid shot a shaft,   [mischievous
>   That play'd a DAME a shavie –   [trick or joke
> The Fiddler RAK'D her, FORE AND AFT,
>   Behint the Chicken cavie: [coop
> Her lord, a wight of HOMER's craft
>   Tho' limpan wi' the Spavie,   [tumoured or
>   handicapped leg
> He hirpl'd up an' lap like daft,   [limped; leapt
>   An' shor'd them DAINTY DAVIE   [offered
>   O' *boot* that night.

(ll. 190–98)

Female licentiousness, then, is as to the fore as the male variety. The women's regular lover among the assembly is a singer of ballads following in the footsteps of Homer, 'the eldest ballad singer on record' (according to Burns's footnote). Cuckolded he may be judged to be, but his own philosophy casts doubt on the meaningfulness of this as he sings a general song of love to his primitive art and to women:

> Great love I bear to all the FAIR,
>   Their humble slave an' a' that;
> But lordly WILL, I hold it still
>   A mortal sin to thraw that.   [frustrate

In raptures sweet this hour we meet,
Wi' mutual love an' a' that;
But for how lang the FLIE MAY STANG,   [fly; sting
Let INCLINATION law that.

(ll. 220–27)

On the face of it, we have here a world turned upside down
where institutions such as rank and monogamy are undercut by
natural status. Even the language of romantic love, such as 'their
humble slave', is undercut with the offhand shorthand of 'an' a'
that'. As David Daiches has said of these lines, 'the entire
Petrarchan tradition of love poetry is implicitly dismissed'.[3] The
official world is viewed as habitually hypocritical in language
and institution by the balladeer, who 'never drank the MUSES'
STANK' (l. 216) and prefers instead simply alcohol, and who
ends the cantata with a joyous cry of iconoclasm:

Here's to BUDGETS, BAGS and WALLETS!   [leather bags
Here's to all the wandering train!
Here's our ragged BRATS and CALLETS!   [wenches
One and all cry out, AMEN!
A fig for those by LAW protected,
LIBERTY's a glorious feast!
COURTS for Cowards were erected,
CHURCHES built to please the Priest.

(ll. 274–81)

Burns's appropriation of the term 'Liberty' here from the usual
context of the respectable rubrics of British and American
constitutional theory, and his framing it within beggar litera-
ture, marks out a fairly unusual literary stance, though one, as
Thomas Crawford has written, consonant with a new appre-
hension of 'general European squalor and a general European
energy of which Rousseau and Blake, each in his own way, were
also aware'.[4]

We see Burns's warping of 'official' political rhetoric again in
'The Rights of Woman – Spoken by Miss Fontenelle on Her
Benefit Night' (PS 390), which represents an interesting
variation on the theme of 'Poor Bodies Do Naething But M-w':

WHILE Europe's eye is fixed on mighty things,
The fate of Empires, and the fall of Kings;
While quacks of State must each produce his plan,

And every children lisp The Rights of Man;
Amid this mighty fuss, just let me mention,
The Rights of Woman merit some attention.

(ll. 1–6)

Whether Burns had read Mary Wollstonecraft's *Vindication of the Rights of Woman* (1792) or not, his poem has little to do with this work. Why bother with politics when the delights of women are there to take the attention of men, the poem asks? The 'rights' of females, as adumbrated by Burns, are 'protection' (l. 8), 'decorum' in treatment (l. 16) and 'admiration' (l. 28), all of these being qualities to be proffered to womankind by the male of the species. In a final movement the poem appropriates the language of revolutionary France to urge this true business of life:

But truce with kings, and truce with Constitutions,
With bloody armaments, and Revolutions;
Let MAJESTY your first attention summon,
Ah, ça ira! THE MAJESTY OF WOMAN!!!

(ll. 35–8)

Allegedly there was alarm caused by Burns's leading the cry of 'ça ira' at the playhouse in Dumfries and so his revolutionary tendency. It may be, however, that this gossip had its origins in the words he put into Louisa Fontenelle's mouth, an actress who spoke the lines above as a player at Dumfries. If so, this is a very ironic situation. As so often in Burnsian biography and work, 'worldly' concerns are put aside in his admiration for an attractive woman. It is clear that he was greatly enamoured of Fontenelle, writing another poem addressed to her, one of his poorer efforts, the gushing 'On seeing Miss Fontenelle in a Favourite Character', and an excitedly sycophantic and self-pitying letter to the actress in November 1792, the intended effect of which, it is clear, was to attract Fontenelle to him.

Another part of the poem's context, according to Burns's nineteenth-century editors Chambers and Wallace, was Burns's disgust at the Caledonian Hunt at Dumfries, an annual round of partying by the county aristocracy set. Though Burns does complain in a letter of 1794 about this event's 'roar of Folly & Dissipation' (*L* ii. 321), there is no direct evidence that he had this in mind when writing 'The Rights of Woman'. In the reading of the poem by Chambers and Wallace, Burns is implicitly satirizing the debauchery of the Caledonian Hunt by counterpointing this with the sentimental rhetoric of the eighteenth century subscribed to so hypocritically by the social elite. This is a somewhat attractive reading, reiterated by subsequent Burns criticism, but it probably underestimates the extent to which Burns in the piece is almost wholly focused upon making an impression on a pretty young actress. Nonetheless, Burns's wielding of the rhetoric of sentimental protectiveness towards woman, however barbed or unbarbed this was in intention, highlights interesting sites of complication in the poet. Is he fundamentally a poet of the 'age of sentiment', subscribing primarily to polite social sensibility (which many of his utterances elsewhere most certainly indicate), or is he the licentious libertarian to which much of his work surveyed above points? Similarly, we might ask if Burns is someone passionately engaged with political philosophy, as much twentieth-century criticism has argued, or if he is cynical, either personally on occasion when he has more carnal interests at heart, or because of a deeper, wider sense of cultural alienation from the processes of political argument, pointed to in the withering sketch of the European regimes in 'Poor Bodies Do Naething But M-w' or in the cheapened currency (if that is what the poet is peddling) of democratic rhetoric in 'The Rights of Woman'. The reading of 'The Rights of Woman' by Chambers and Wallace is borne out of their knowledge that Burns certainly was in favour of thinkers such as those who had helped form the mentality of the French Revolution, including Thomas Paine (whose *Rights of Man* was also the inspiration for Wollstonecraft's proto-feminist tract). Despite the best efforts of critics to harmonize Burns's attitudes into a single cogent, coherent outlook, however, it is perhaps time to recognize that the man and his work do, indeed, represent contradictions that remain irresolvable. Burns the artist, living at a time of such huge cultural ferment in the western world, adopts a range of roles and personae, both consciously and (to some extent, perhaps when his personal goals are not necessarily consonant with the large principles he would wish otherwise to exemplify) unconsciously. Recognition of such complexity is a prerequisite to the normalization of our perception of Burns as neither an absolute reprobate nor an untrammelled, superhuman political animal, both tendencies that have historically afflicted commentary on Burns.

One of Burns's strangest and most celebrated real-life relationships with a woman is with Agnes McLehose (1758–1841), who was estranged from her husband when Burns met her in Edinburgh during his lionization there in 1787. That this relationship was expressed through a series of fervent letters, rather than through overt sexual activity, provides another area of psycho-textual intrigue in Burns's life and work. After a brief meeting for the first time at a tea party in December 1787, a more private interview was proposed by McLehose but was delayed when Burns severely sprained his leg. From a convalescence that took up much of his limited remaining time in the Scottish capital, the poet wrote to her:

> I cannot bear the idea of leaving Edinburgh without seeing you. I know not how to account for it – I am strangely taken with some people, nor am I often mistaken. You are a stranger to me; – but I am an odd being. Some yet unnamed feelings – things, not principles, but better than whims – carry me further than boasted reason ever did a philosopher. (*LL* 2)

Here we see Burns inhabiting his sentimental 'heaven-taught ploughman' persona, but, interestingly, the poet is not simply affecting this stance in the selfish pursuit of a woman. Rather, he is engaging in something more complex. As Carol McGuirk has observed of the beginnings of the friendship, 'even in a description of Agnes M'Lehose to Captain Richard Brown, an old comrade in dissipation to whom Burns might have been expected to unbend a little, Burns still introduces the topic of his new flirtation with a literary allusion, and assumes a familiar sentimental pose in describing the relationship'.[5] Aside from a considerable personal attraction between the couple, Burns was very aware that each of them occupied in their own way an awkward social space. The sexual electricity in their correspondence and in their face-to-face dealings cannot be gainsaid, but both embark upon a process of legitimizing their friendship through the wielding of discourses that act as impeccable shields against any suggestion of impropriety. At the most obvious level this happens in Burns's third letter to McLehose, where he begins to utilize for himself and his correspondent the

pastoral names of 'Sylvander' and 'Clarinda' (a device appar-
ently suggested by McLehose in a letter lost in manuscript).
Paradoxically, in the same epistle he writes:

> I don't know if you have a just idea of my character, but I wish you
> to see me as I am. I am, as most people of my trade are, a strange
> Will-o'-wisp being; the victim, too frequently, of much imprudence,
> and many follies. My great constituent elements are pride and
> passion: the first I have endeavoured to humanize into integrity and
> honour; the last makes me a devotee, to the warmest degree of
> enthusiasm, in love, religion, or friendship: either of them, or
> altogether, as I happen to be inspired. (LL 7)

Agnes responded as 'Clarinda' on the evening of the same day
to the seeming confessional candour of this passage with a
project in mind: 'Religion, the only refuge of the unfortunate,
has been my balm in every woe. O! could I make her appear to
you as she has done to me! Instead of ridiculing her tenets, you
would fall down and worship her very semblance wherever you
found it!' (LL 9). As Burns is reinventing McLehose as the
pastoral heroine, a role for which society in viewing her status as
an estranged wife would have judged her entirely unfit, so
McLehose decides that she will seek to persuade Burns to be
more regulated by true religion. The 'ridiculing' of religion by
Burns to which McLehose refers is primarily with regard to 'The
Holy Fair', one of the most popular pieces of both the
Kilmarnock and the Edinburgh editions of Burns's poetry.
McLehose, intense in her Presbyterian outlook, is one of many
individuals enraptured by the initial publication of Burns's
work, yet also troubled by aspects of it.

The extent to which Burns and McLehose go along with the
attempts of the one to remould the other and their desire to be
somehow unified are very evident. Clarinda begins to write
poetry, and, in a similarly chameleon-like transaction, Burns in
response to receiving this verse inhabits the language of
religion. On 3 January 1788 he wrote to her, 'Your last verses
have so delighted me, that I have copied them in among some of
my own most valued pieces, which I keep sacred for my own
use' (LL 14). Here we have nothing less than a symbolic marriage
between the pair, textually consummated the following day,
when Burns makes alterations to one of her pieces three stanzas
long concerning unrequited love, saying that he has found a

suitable tune and intends to publish them in the recently begun *Scots Musical Museum*, of which he was the principal compiler, after Clarinda has added a fourth stanza for which he saw a necessity. Sylvander, however, spoils the momentum by himself providing in a 'p.s' a possible fourth stanza, the words of which have been torn from the manuscript of the letter, most probably by Clarinda, embarrassed by expressions in it she presumably thought to be too direct with regard to their personal liaison. Clarinda replied to Sylvander with a mixture of appreciating suffusion and a renewed attempt to recall to her penfriend the prior claims of God and religion over the will of human beings. In turn Burns writes back with an emotionally charged admiration for her 'enthusiasm for religion' (*LL* 21), and the subsequent and lengthy correspondence between the pair is marked by a to and fro of both highly charged religious and pastoral sentiment, periodically forcing Clarinda to upbraid her correspondent when he speaks too plainly of their shared feelings for one another. In the letters, Sylvander is recurrently forced back upon his cunning linguistic strategy of mixing rhetorics in the spheres of passion and spirit. We see this, for instance, as Sylvander writes, 'My likings are both strong and eternal' (*LL* 26). In another guileful moment, Sylvander responds to Clarinda's reminders that they should be careful with their thoughts about one another, 'Oh, I have sins to heaven, but none to you' (*LL* 29). Despite the speculations of some biographers, the relationship probably never became physical (Burns during his early liaison with 'Clarinda', in fact, was conducting a relationship with a servant-girl, Jenny Clow, whom he made pregnant). Instead the intercourse between the two consisted of fervent communication in person as well as in their letters. In another early letter Clarinda writes to Sylvander of one exquisite conversation that had passed between the pair: 'I will not deny it, Sylvander, last night was one of the most exquisite I ever experienced. Few such fall to the lot of mortals! Few, extremely few, are formed to relish such refined enjoyment. That it should be so, vindicates the wisdom of Heaven' (*LL* 30).

If Burns was frustrated in his inability to go beyond words with McLehose, he seems never to have stopped enjoying the verbal froth that the pair inspired in one another. During 1788 he contributed a brace of items to the *Scots Musical Museum* on

Clarinda, the first of these providing an opening line, 'Clarinda, mistress of my soul', that has a stronger than usual purchase within the received, standard sentiment, given the probably impregnable piety of the real-life addressee. Burns continued to correspond with McLehose until 1792, with her responses becoming eventually less frequent and enthusiastic as she moved towards a rapprochement with her husband and in the end announced her plan to leave to live with her spouse in Jamaica. In anticipation of this event, Burns penned 'Ae Fond Kiss', one of the most famous love songs in the Scots or English languages. Once again, this respectable staple of the Burns canon rests, like 'To a Louse', on a larger hinterland of work from Burns's reserved canon. In this instance, the private correspondence between Sylvander and Clarinda is, of course, not explicitly sexual, unlike 'Love and Liberty' or *The Merry Muses*, but it was far from being full of propriety so far as institutional society was concerned. Thomas Stewart, the Glasgow printer, fraudulently obtained and published some of the correspondence in 1801 and 1802, and helped precipitate a long-standing bourgeois horror during the nineteenth century at Burns's involvement with a woman from a higher social caste than himself. Like the gamekeeper in *Lady Chatterley's Lover*, Burns's offence was not so much against sex as class. Burns the iconoclast of society rather than the body is what should finally be emphasized.

6

Folk Culture

The rather artificial construction of 'Burns the bard' sits somewhat at odds with Burns's true relationship to what is called today 'folk culture'. The literati who hailed Burns as the 'heaven-taught ploughman' were actually complicit in a literary construct more to do with the age of sensibility when primitivism and the idea of the noble savage held sway, rather than simply receptive to genuinely untutored expression. Burns's folk culture encompassed bawdry, which he was careful not to present undiluted to the majority of his public, and 'folk songs', some of which he made more genteel in accordance with the tastes of the day. When commenting on the mores of the Ayrshire peasantry, Burns applied an Enlightenment anthropological lens, which again shows us the limited truth in Burns's often alleged 'directness' of, or simply 'realistic', expression. Truly, from an early age, Burns had imbibed family and regional culture that was not exactly in the cultural mainstream. His father's origins in the north-east, a strong Jacobite area in which some of the Burneses had been 'out' in support of the Stuarts in the early eighteenth century certainly contributed to Burns's interest in Jacobite song (though this seems to have been primarily a personal, imaginative choice rather than as a result of any direct support from his immediate family of 'Whiggish' Presbyterians). Also, it should be remembered that Jacobite song was often the work of a Tory, aristocratic class which became only from the late eighteenth century (and in large part because of Burns's influence) a staple part of a generalized Scottish 'folk' canon. Burns's love of song more generally, and love songs in particular, was first imbibed from his mother, Agnes Broun, who knew many old ballads. As well as 'modernizing' old Scottish songs, Burns also collected and preserved many such works, broadcasting these in such a way as to participate in the 'folk' revival that is one of the strong energies of the emerging Romantic period. From an old female servant of the Burnes family the poet also inherited a store of old supernatural stories, and these no doubt played a formative part in his imagination.

'Native' oral influences on Burns, however, have to be balanced with the influence of Burns's reading. This is certainly true of Burns's two 'supernatural' poems in the Kilmarnock edition, 'Address to the Deil' (*PS* 76) and 'Halloween' (*PS* 73). 'Address to the Deil' takes its cue from Burns's reading of Milton's Satan, in an epigraph from *Paradise Lost* on the majesty of Satan leading his forces into battle. In dialogue with Milton's epic, Burns presents instead a burlesque pointing out in his opening stanza that Satan is, indeed (as the received iconography of overlordship dictates), multi-titled. But in this case the welter of titles is to be found in the folk-sphere: 'O THOU, whatever title suits thee! / Auld Hornie, Satan, Nick, or Clootie' (ll. 1–2), the last epithet, the name for a cloven hoof, especially localizing the depiction of the Devil in the countryside. The bathos continues as the narrator wonders why Satan should be interested in the common folk:

> Hear me, *auld Hangie*, for a wee,
> An' let poor, *damned bodies* bee;
> I'm sure sma' pleasure it can gie,
>   Ev'n to a *deil*,
> To skelp an' scaud poor dogs like me,   [scald
>   An' hear us squeel!
>
> (ll. 7–12)

The contradictory activity of Satan is cumulatively humorous as, on the one hand, and as in Scripture, he is viewed 'ranging like a roaring lion' (l. 19), and on the other, hiding in 'holes an' corners' (l. 20), waiting to pounce on the unwary. Interestingly, Burns is here sceptical in note, when an orthodox Christian and, indeed, folk reading of Satan would take cognizance of the Devil's shape-shifting abilities. We begin to realize in Burns's poem that Satan is a scapegoat for human incapability, including cases of impotence, where his agent-witches will cast spells and use charms bringing about such misfortune:

Thence, mystic knots mak great abuse,
On *Young-Guidmen*, fond, keen an' croose; [cocksure
When the best *warklum* i' the house, [worktool (here,
figuratively, the penis)
   By cantraip wit, [magic
Is instant made no worth a louse,
   Just at the bit.

(ll. 61–6)

This unmistakable innuendo, where the idea of a weaver's loom is
rendered inoperable ('just at the bit'), is a favourite strategy of
Burns, as we have seen in 'The Court of Equity', where the man's
trade is conjoined with his sexual function. It is another moment
that Hugh Blair wanted to excise for the Edinburgh edition, when
one might have expected the Christian minister to object to the
supernatural scepticism in general in the poem. What is revealed
once again, it would seem, is the rather strange 'polite' Enlight-
enment culture into which Burns was received, his somewhat
irreligious sensibility permissible but his scatology disallowed.

Burns teases credulous perception again when he alludes to
the reputation for mysticism among freemasonry of which he
was a member. A young 'brother' is pictured being whipped off
to hell as the craft unwisely summon up Satan at a meeting.
Here Burns ironically plays along with the superstition of the
common folk in seeing Masonry as diabolic when, in fact, it was
more often to do with being self-consciously (rationally)
cultured. It ought to be seen as encompassing Enlightenment
rationality, a strong part of which was the enjoyment by men
such as Burns in being able with untroubled mind to be part of a
secret society supposedly possessing arcane knowledge. Free-
masons in Burns's time (including the likes of Mozart), in fact,
were often discussing the most advanced ideas in politics and in
thought generally, and we perhaps see such an idea when, after
a profusion of comedy, 'Address to the Deil' ends on a
surprisingly sober note, where sympathy is extended to Satan:

But fare ye weel, auld *Nickie-ben!*
O wad ye tak a thought an' men'!
Ye aiblins might – I dinna ken – [perhaps
   Still hae a *stake* –
I'm wae to think upo' yon den,
Ev'n for your sake.

(ll. 121–6)

The narrator wishes that even Satan might be saved from hell, and we realize that the poem has been, as much as anything, a catalogue of human petty-mindedness or blame attribution. 'Evil' has been laughed at not out of simple religious scepticism, but because too often it comes from within rather than from without. The narrator's final gesture, hoping that some good might come of the Devil, is a suitably powerful corrective to a human world that frequently extends no sympathy even to its own kind.

'Halloween' is by far Burns's most extensively annotated poem in the Kilmarnock edition. Its introductory note explains that its principal theme, the folk belief in foretelling the future 'may be some entertainment to a philosophic mind, if any such should honor the Author with a perusal, to see the remains of it, among the more unenlightened in our own'. The poem is then prefaced with an epigraph taken from Goldsmith's *The Deserted Village*, commending 'the simple pleasures of the lowly train'. Burns's opening of the poem itself presents us with a mostly dignified scene of folk customs in the 'Christ's Kirk' stanza that has two strong prototypes in the Scots poetic tradition, Fergusson's 'Hallow-Fair' (1772) and John Mayne's 'Halloween' (1780). 'Halloween', it is apparent, is another of Burns's polyvocal performances where the enlightened antiquarian persona is to the fore in the poem, but denied absolute authority in the subtextual materials and the respectful exuberance of the main poetic text itself. Traditional readings of Burns might see him marked by a 'crisis of identity' in such a diverse configuration of materials, but we need not straitjacket Burns in this fashion. Instead, we might read the epigraph from Goldsmith showing Burns's controlled acknowledgement that there is more than one way of 'looking' at the customs he is about to describe. The poet who in 'The Holy Fair' reveals a more 'natural' ritualistic sensibility in the peasantry struggling to free itself from that prescribed by the church, here gives full vent to the ritual of courtship and community in such a way as to paint a peasant dignity that gainsays the condescending antiquarian voice that introduces the poem:

> The lasses feat, an' cleanly neat   [spruce
>   Mair braw than when they're fine;

83

Their faces blythe, fu' sweetly kythe,   [happy; make known
  Hearts leal, an' warm, an' kin':   [leal
The lads sae trig, wi' wooer-babs,   [neat; love knots
  Weel knotted on their garten,
Some unco blate, an' some wi' gabs,   [shy; mouths
  Gar lasses hearts gang startin
      Whyles fast at night.

(ll. 19–27)

What we see in this text is not so much a tension in Burns himself, as that fruitful fissure in Enlightenment thinking that, from a basis of rationalistic principle, sought to explore 'primitive' mores and began to find not simply that which was to be expurgated, but a 'superstition' that was often culturally, or even 'socially' (to use a watchword of the Enlightenment), meaningful. Gently humorous, Burns's poem describes folk-practices for obtaining something that a person desires, finding the name of a true love, and foretelling marriage, among others, all of which show the concerns of the peasantry to be the same essential material and emotional desires pursued elsewhere by others. Burns's celebration of these mores emerges from an Enlightenment anthropological mindset and is set in literary form by the poet's immersion in Goldsmith and also, again, the poets of the Scots tradition who are primarily north-east and non-Presbyterian in cultural origin. Burns imports the dignified literary presentation of the peasantry found in Goldsmith, Fergusson and Mayne to Ayrshire, where the Calvinist church, for all its puritanical proclivities, has clearly not extirpated such local customs. These customs, however, were not celebrated in poetry in Ayrshire before Burns, and so we see the poet once again extending the literary space of his native region.

Burns's folk essays in poetry (among which we might number a wide variety of poems such as 'The Holy Fair', 'The Twa Dogs', 'The Cotter's Saturday Night' and 'Love and Liberty', as well as 'Halloween' and 'Address to the Deil') are added to in the Edinburgh edition of the following year with two main items. 'The Ordination' is a close-focus view of the named individuals involved in intellectual battles between evangelicals and moderates over the accession to the ministry of the Laigh Kirk in Kilmarnock in 1785, which, like 'Holy Willie's Prayer', Burns saw prudence in omitting from his first collection. If 'Holy

Willie's Prayer' was also left out of the Edinburgh edition, largely at the behest of literary advisers such as Hugh Blair who saw it as too overwhelmingly crude, 'The Ordination', clearly, was a piece Burns now felt confident in placing before the public, immune from any malice that might rebound on him for treating with cavalier humour the personnel of local church politics of Ayrshire in even more explicit detail than he had done in 'The Holy Fair'.

A much more accomplished addition to Burns's 'folk' canon in the Edinburgh edition, however, is 'Death and Doctor Hornbook. A True Story' (*PS* 55) which, amid its broad comedy, is a poem thoughtfully apprehensive about human confidence in progress. The poem satirizes the branching-out of a schoolteacher at Tarbolton, John Wilson (a man with whom the poet remained on good terms), into the selling of chemical substances to effect medical cures, a huge growth-area in the late eighteenth century. A drunken narrator meets Death, and so is understandably frightened but also belligerent:

> It spak right howe – 'My name is *Death*,   [deep
> 'But be na' fley'd.' – Quoth I, 'Guid faith,   [frightened
> 'Ye're maybe come to stap my breath;
>   'But tent me, billie;   [chap
> 'I red ye weel, tak care o' skaith,   [harm
>   'See there's a gully!'   [large knife

(ll. 49–54)

This threat to stab Death is ridiculous, of course, but mirrors the activities of Dr Hornbook, whose knowledge is making him equally defiant of the Grim Reaper in his curing of people at an unnatural rate. Death provides the narrator with a catalogue of Hornbook's activities, glad to have the chance of some friendly conversation in his currently depressed condition. The serious point being made is that human science is somewhat sinister in its remaking of the conditions of life and death. It is on this basis that Death presents Hornbook, in a nice inversion (so typical of Burns) of the usual categories of reality, as an uncanny creature practising a kind of perverted magic. Hornbook, Death hints, is even a corrupter of morals and a murderer to boot, as his 'medicine' also has been used very conveniently to remove a useless wife:

'An honest Wabster to his trade,   [weaver
'Whase wife's twa nieves were scarce weel-bred,   [fists
'Gat tippence-worth to mend her head,
    'When it was sair;
'The wife slade cannie to her bed,   [slipped; wisely
    'But ne'er spak mair.'

(ll. 151–6)

Natural death, then, is now being usurped by man's rude interference in the process of the life cycle. Seemingly a comic squib in form, 'Death and Doctor Hornbook' nonetheless expresses a fear of the darkness (in the 'modern' period as much as in any earlier, supposedly more 'primitive' time) of human nature, with its potential to do more damage than any 'supernatural' creature.

Burns's greatest folk-essay, arguably his poetic masterpiece, is 'Tam o' Shanter. A Tale' (1790; *PS* 321). However, the notion of the poem as based upon a 'popular tale' has dogged the text. Apart from the ubiquitous 'wild ride' aspect in the context of folklore it is far from clear what particular source, if any, Burns had in mind for his poem. Burns in a letter to Francis Grose during the summer of 1790 provided several stories of diabolic doings surrounding Alloway Kirk that loosely inform 'Tam o' Shanter', and which, in their diffuse collective, speak of no particularly cogent local folk tradition *prior* to Burns's composition of his poem. No doubt the ruins of Alloway Kirk did excite local superstition, but Burns, in a sense, was playing to the gallery. The poem appears in its first published form in the *Edinburgh Magazine* for March 1791, and, more importantly, one month later in volume two of Captain Grose's *Antiquities of Scotland*. In the second of these contexts it forms part of a rather odd item. Amid a survey of the much more venerable ruins of abbeys and castles in the book Alloway Kirk is very small beer. Its insertion as a location of historical curiosity is really an excuse for Grose's drinking crony, Burns, to parade his fine poem. Grose provides a very short and vague description of the ruin at Alloway, the most salient point of which is to say that 'it is one of the eldest parishes in Scotland', which is to say nothing at all. In a limp footnote to his discourse, Grose says of the kirk, 'the church is also famous for being wherein the witches and warlocks used to hold their meetings'.[1] In an even larger sense than 'Halloween', then, we have a text where the antiquarian voice (belonging to someone other than Burns) has its authority somewhat undermined. The text of 'Tam o' Shanter', itself a (very large) footnote to Grose's description, is *in toto* a kind of staged overexcited response to the real, physical scene which Grose's book ostensibly surveys. Here there is a pointer to the thematic texture of the poem itself, which consists of the trammelled interface between the real world and the dark, emotional inner spaces of the human mind. A mock epic, certainly, the text combines with its comedy a psychological investigation that yet again marks out the Enlightenment credentials of Burns.

The poem is rather duplicitous from the outset as it peddles a humble scene in highly poised couplets, which are sustained across a particularly long and elegant unit of sense:

WHEN chapman billies leave the street,	[pedlars
And drouthy neebors, neebors meet,	[thirsty
As market-days are wearing late,	
An' folk begin to tak the gate;	
While we sit bousing at the nappy,	[boozing; ale
And getting fou and unco happy,	[full; uncommonly
We think na on the lang Scots miles,	
The mosses, waters, slaps, and styles,	[gaps in dykes
That lie between us and our hame,	
Whare sits our sulky sullen dame,	
Gathering her brows like gathering storm,	
Nursing her wrath to keep it warm.	

(ll. 1–12)

The movement here from the male cronyism, the husband out drinking, to the solitary female, the wife sitting at home, defines one of the 'real' distances the poem is describing, as opposed to the actually less important physical distance that the poem's eponymous character has to traverse on his way home through supernatural forces. The poem essays, in fact, male irresponsibility and 'fear' of the female, rather than fear of any more mysterious unknown. The opening lines of the poem telescope the idea of the supernatural and the ordinary wife who is almost possessed, in the mind of a husband at least, of a power over the elements as she gathers 'her brows like gathering storm'. Given Burns's reputation with the opposite sex, we have here another instance where he revealingly punctures the male psyche. Tam's perception of his wife, Kate, in the face of his habitual drinking excesses renders her witch-like, as a torrent of deprecatory, almost incanting, words are poured on him from her direction: 'She tauld thee weel thou was a skellum [scoundrel], / A blethering, blustering, drunken blellum [blusterer]' (ll. 19–20). Rather than spend time with his wife, Tam chooses to fritter the night with another woman, the barmaid 'Kirkton Jean', and this is one of several points in the poem where male immaturity and even irrationality is located. An apostrophizing narrative voice points to the distance that a man such as Tam seems intent on placing between himself and his wife:

> Ah, gentle dames! it gars me greet, [makes; weep
> To think how mony counsels sweet,
> How mony lengthen'd sage advices,
> The husband frae the wife despises!
>
> (ll. 33–6)

Here the sententious voice is humorously undercut with immediate effect, as the notion of 'a man of feeling' (a narrator who is reduced to tears by what he observes) is contradicted by the low-style Scots word 'greet'. The narrator here is seemingly complicit in a 'nudge-nudge, wink-wink' fashion with the male point of view as he expresses the responsible (or 'official') outlook in tongue-in-cheek fashion. The blatant irony of the narrator, however, is itself exploded in its smugness by the end of the poem.

The narrator seemingly takes leave of his 'moralizing' with a peremptory 'But to our tale' (l. 37), and begins to describe Tam o' Shanter drinking one night to excess with his friend Souter (or Cobbler) Johnny: '*Tam* lo'ed him like a vera brither' (l. 43). We are, then, moved safely back into the male space where Tam's 'dame' cannot touch him: 'The storm without might rair and rustle, / *Tam* did na mind the storm a whistle' (ll. 51–2). Simultaneously here, along with the gender comedy where storm and wife waiting at home are conjoined, there is tenderness as well as laughter being directed towards Tam. The 'whistle' refers to the humble music and chatter with which Tam and his compatriots at the inn surround themselves. There is a defiant but fragile quality to their revelry, and this nice ambivalence paves the way for a raising up of the humble farmer Tam in the language of natural description and of metaphysical location as Tam's drunken emotion is described:

> As bees flee hame wi' lades o' treasure,
> The minutes wing'd their way wi' pleasure:
> Kings may be blest, but *Tam* was glorious,
> O'er a' the ills o' life victorious!

(ll. 55–8)

We have here a kind of narrative duplicity as Tam's mood is both collaborated with and measured through these similes and found to be inflated. The narrator, then, both sympathizes with and mildly mocks Tam. If we are beginning to see the poem pointing to its mock-epic nature where Tam is such a humble protagonist, he is also a universal representative of human nature, both as amply human and as fragile as any king. A series of metaphors is used to garland Tam's situation:

> But pleasures are like poppies spread,
> You seize the flower, its bloom is shed;
> Or like the snow falls in the river,
> A moment white – then melts forever;
> Or like the borealis race,
> That flit ere you can point their place;
> Or like the rainbow's lovely form
> Evanishing amid the storm.

(ll. 59–66)

Some critics have read these lines, full of Augustan *sententia*, as inappropriate to a protagonist such as Tam and so simply inserted for comical effect. However, we might suggest that we see instead an instance of the democratization of literature, typical of the emerging Romantic age, where the small man is entitled to his adventure and his poetic language as much as anyone.

We have not quite embarked upon 'our tale' as the narrator has promised. The story has been resisted as Tam's mood and situation have been subjected to a leisurely consideration more usually appropriate to characters, of either greater status or more complex mental processes, conventionally to be exulted. Eventually, however, Tam must leave his pleasant company and take the road home. He is exposed to the elements in a passage

89

arranged with huge skill, the rhythms of which mimic Tam's galloping along on his mare and the assonance of which mimics his anxious gulping, in response to both the buffeting by the elements and his foreboding of other forces:

> The wind blew as 'twad blawn its last;
> The rattling showers rose on the blast;
> The speedy gleams the darkness swallow'd;
> Loud, deep, and lang, the thunder bellow'd:
> That night, a child might understand,
> The Deil had business on his hand.

(ll. 73–8)

We have rapidly moved, then, from the terrain of mature (or adult) philosophical poetry to a fearfulness associated with childish ghost-stories. Again the uncertainty of human discourse and of human moods is pointed to. The effect, certainly, is comical, but something complex is being said also about the human mind. We have a rational or philosophical capacity where we can reflect on or codify our situation to *understand* that we are fragile creatures. We have also, however, an irrational capacity where we *feel* our vulnerability. The childish or superstitious ghost-legends that begin to form in Tam's mind are, in their own way, as accurate an index of the standing of the individual in a world over which he has very little control as the august metaphors of 'art' poetry that come to the same conclusion. Tam is pictured proceeding on a journey that is briefly as elementally heroic as that of any Homeric protagonist: 'Tam skelpit on thro' dub [puddle] and mire, / Despising wind, and rain, and fire' (ll. 81–2). Measured irony remains, however, in that Tam is mentally fearful as he gallops through the night with a purposefulness showing that physically he is courageous enough. The greatest fears, as so often the case in the human situation, are caused by the operations of an overactive mind. We might read the poem as proposing that very often humans think too much (which is why Tam's largely thoughtless revelry, or necessary release, in the pub is to be laughed at but is far from entirely condemned). Tam's courage, in fact, grows the longer he remains unmolested by anything untoward emerging at him from the night. Indeed he begins, perhaps, even to enjoy remembrance of the sinister goings on associated in incidents and tales with his environment that come fast and thick in his mind:

By this time he was cross the ford,
Whare, in the snaw, the chapman smoor'd;   [smothered
And past the birks and meikle stane,   [birches; large stone
Whare drunken *Charlie* brak's neck-bane;
And thro' the whins, and by the cairn,   [gorses
Whare hunters fand the murder'd bairn;   [found
And near the thorn, aboon the well,
Where *Mungo*'s mither hang'd hersel.

(ll. 89–96)

We have something of a mirror effect here, where just as the reader is enjoying Tam's tale with all its portents pointing to an uncanny encounter we know will come, so too Tam is consuming the same kind of material. We share a prurient attitude with Tam that is a ubiquitous feature in human nature. Here, as elsewhere in the poem, we are being told implicitly that Tam and we are alike. As we enjoy this poem we are not so very different in our outlook from a 'superstitious peasant'. The cultured, literate reader 'appealed' to, perhaps laughing at Tam, when reading lines 55–66 quoted above, is not so distanced from Tam's mentality as he or she might like to think. As he plays with kinds of story-telling, mixing art poetry and folk story, Burns shows that he knew very well that he was catering for an increasingly mainstream cultural taste for folklore. He makes creative capital from a tension in this taste that his own work's reception and consumption allowed him to know better than anyone during his age. It is in 'Tam 'o Shanter' that Burns utilizes this tension for consummate creative capital as he is, at last, fully sceptical of a cultural hierarchy to which he had paid lip-service for so long.

Tam's new-found courage (mirroring, we might say, Burns's courage in painting the fullest folk scene he has ever attempted) is rewarded as he dismounts at the old church of Alloway in response to activity there, and is treated to the sight of an orgy. The conviviality that he witnesses, where warlocks and witches dance while Satan in the shape of a beast plays the pipes, parallels the hospitable scene that Tam has left at the pub:

Coffins stood round, like open presses,   [cupboards
That shaw'd the dead in their last dresses;
And by some devilish cantraip slight   [magic; skill
Each in its cauld hand held a light. –
By which heroic *Tam* was able
To note upon the haly table,
A murderer's banes in gibbet airns;   [irons
Twa span-lang, wee, unchristen'd bairns,
A thief, new cutted frae a rape,
Wi' his last gasp his gab did gape;   [mouth
Five tomahawks, wi' blude red-rusted;
Five scymitars, wi' murder crusted;
A garter, which a babe had strangled;
A knife, a father's throat had mangled,
Whom his ain son o' life bereft,
The grey hairs yet stack to the heft;   [handle
Wi' mair o' horrible and awefu'
Which even to name wad be unlawfu'.

(ll. 125–42)

Ironically, Tam is back to being 'heroic' as he has felt himself to be in the pub, as he looks on a scene that entertains rather than horrifies him. The catalogue of curiosities, including the alien tomahawks and scimitars (read about in cheap chapbook literature of the period), perhaps tells us that it is Tam's imagination that is creating the scene, rather than the actually demonic. Similarly, we ought to be aware that the location of Alloway Kirk as a suitable scene of demonic activity is the result of cultural conditioning. Alloway Kirk's reputation as a place of dark goings-on has to do with the superseding of this church-site as a place of Catholic worship with the Reformation and the building of a new church beside it to supplant a place associated in the Scottish Presbyterian mindset with the Antichrist. Both the place in general itself, featured in Grose's *Antiquities of Scotland*, and the contents of this chamber of horrors are not simply of interest to Tam, of course, but to the 'modern' and 'educated' readership that Burns is very well aware of possessing. He teases this reader as the narrator ends his list by saying that there are even greater enormities that he dare not name because simply to do so would be against the law. One might well wonder, however, what could be even more repugnant than the infanticide and so on that has already been named. We have here, perhaps, satire upon the appetite (in the eighteenth century as now) for sensationally scandalous human behaviour. We might notice also that Satan is generally companionable amid the awful scene, and that it is the behaviour of human beings that is altogether more frightening. To some degree, we might read 'Tam o' Shanter' as a poem that says what humans have to be most afraid of are other beings like themselves.

As he watches the dancing, the narrator addresses Tam, saying to him that it is a pity that the scene he is observing consists of ugly hags rather than beautiful young girls. As things stand the narrator wonders how it 'didna turn thy stomach' (l. 162), and so slyly points to a depth of human appetite (for the warped spectacle, at least, even if Tam is not actually sexually excited by the old witches). The voyeur Tam, though, is able to pick out of the scene one very attractive, scantily clad witch, Nannie (who afterwards we are told is responsible for crop failures, the death of beasts and the sinking of boats in the countryside around Carrick). In the face of her, '*Tam* stood, like ane bewitch'd, / And thought his very een [eyes] enrich'd' (ll. 183–4), and so we are aware again of subtle gender psychology in the poem. This woman forms the centre of our awareness of Tam's love–hate relationship with the opposite sex. She has been conjured up out of Tam's frustration at having to go home, leaving behind his sexy hostess who had been arousing him. The young witch also registers, in general, Tam's fear of women, who represent for him both the extremes of responsibility (in the person of Kate, waiting impatiently at home) and his reaction to this in looking (in the pub and in Alloway Kirk) for an alternative, 'dangerous' sexual liaison.[2]

So carried away is our voyeur that he forgets himself completely and shouts out, 'Weel done, Cutty-Sark [short shirt]' (ll. 189). This is an orgasmic moment in a sense and Tam has to 'pay' for his ejaculation (again we have the male fear of being entrapped by women through the sexual act). He is pursued by the hellish legions from the church, and the narrator opines that his poor wife has seen the last of her husband:

> Ah, *Tam*! Ah, *Tam*! thou'll get thy fairin! [reward (worthless
> trinket from a fair)
> In hell they'll roast thee like a herrin!

93

In vain thy *Kate* awaits thy comin!
Kate soon will be a woefu' woman!

(ll. 201–4)

Chased by a largely feminine force he flees towards another feminine location, his wife at home whom he despairs of reaching. He does so, though, as his mare, Maggie (and so another feminine element propelling Tam), manages to leap a stream over which, because of the traditional sanctified nature of fresh water in its association with baptism, the supernatural forces are unable to proceed. Nannie, though, pulls off Maggie's tail as they escape, allowing the narrator to end with a *moralitas*:

> Now, wha this tale o' truth shall read,
> Ilk man and mother's son, take heed: [each
> Whene'er to drink you are inclin'd,
> Or cutty-sarks run in your mind,
> Think, ye may buy the joys o'er dear,
> Remember Tam o' Shanter's mare.

(ll. 219–24)

Burns knows that it is no good warning irresponsible males not to chase women and drink. This is why we have the 'shaggy dog story' ending where the castration symbolism (practised on the tail of a female horse) is mockingly inappropriate. 'Tam o' Shanter' is a poem that laughs indulgently at male folly and knows that it will not be reformed. More widely, it is a poem that sees 'primitive' human behaviour, more generally, not to be something that 'modernity' will simply legislate out of existence. In reaching this conclusion, Burns's poem is one of the most sophisticated 'folk' performances of the late Enlightenment and early Romantic periods.

7

Song

Burns's first written production was the song 'O Once I Lov'd' (*PS* 1), composed in 1774 when the poet was 15. It was a response to being partnered in the communal harvest gathering with another teenager, Nelly Kilpatrick, a girl who charmed Burns with her singing. Later he wrote of his song that it emerged from a time 'when my heart glowed with honest warm simplicity; unacquainted, and uncorrupted with the ways of a wicked world'.[1] What is interesting in both Burns's remark here and in the song itself is the genesis of Burns's expression not in some purely primitive 'folk' context but in a rather 'genteel' (to take a word from 'O Once I Lov'd') folk idiom that was part of the literary mainstream during the eighteenth century. The song's sentiments are identifiably part of a tradition of British pastoral writing found in the work of John Gay and Allan Ramsay, which presents peasants who are impeccably morally conservative:

> But Nelly's looks are blythe and sweet,
> And what is best of a',
> Her reputation is compleat,
> And fair without a flaw;
>
> She dresses ay sae clean and neat,
> Both decent and genteel;
> And then there's something in her gait
> Gars ony dress look weel.

(ll. 13–20)

Burns, of course, was a naive and love-struck young man when he wrote such idealistic words, but the song-writing in which he dabbled for the next ten years was essentially of the same sentimental kind. His first two dozen pieces include versions of the Psalms, pieces forged from the most fashionable sensibility such as 'Song, Composed in August' (*PS* 2) – including the following description of shooting birds:

> Tyrannic man's dominion;
> The Sportsman's joy, the murd'ring cry,
> The flutt'ring, gory pinion!

(ll. 22–4)

which might seem rather overwrought in sensitivity for a working farmer – and highly innocent love songs of standard emotion. Only one of these early pieces, 'Song: It Was upon a Lammas Night' (*PS* 8) comes anywhere near sexual realism while remaining (albeit beautifully) euphemistic:

> I lock'd her in my fond embrace;
>   Her heart was beating rarely:
> My blessings on that happy place,
>   Amang the rigs o' barley!
> But by the moon and stars so bright,
>   That shone that hour so clearly!
> She ay shall bless that happy night,
>   Amang the rigs o' barley.

(ll. 17–24)

For the Kilmarnock edition, Burns followed a well-established pattern for eighteenth-century poets in nodding to pastoral taste by including a few songs towards the end of his volume. As well as the two pieces just cited, he printed a piece in the 'tea-table' or drawing-room genre, 'Song: From Thee, Eliza, I Must Go', and 'The Farewell', a song celebrating his Masonic brotherhood. These are, then, very removed from those songs of Burns's reserved canon 'The Fornicator' or 'Love and Liberty'. Burns was dissuaded from publishing the latter in the Edinburgh edition, and probably he had only fleetingly thought of including the sequence anyway since, by and large, his presentation of song remained essentially unchanged in tenor in the Edinburgh editions of both 1787 and 1793. The 'Green Grow the Rashes' that appears in these editions of his work is, in its gender commentary, wittier than any other song published in these places, but apart from this nothing challenging in sentiment or world view is allowed to intrude. There is instead another publishing location, besides the 'unofficial' chapbook contexts of 'Love and Liberty' and *The Merry Muses*, where Burns is allowed, 'officially' as it were, to be heterodox, experimental and inconsistent. This is the case in the two major song anthologies with which Burns was associated.

The majority of Burns's 373 songs are first published in the *Scots Musical Museum* (1787–1803) conceived by James Johnston which Burns largely edited, and George Thomson's *A Select Collection of Original Scotish Airs* (with contributions from the poet from 1792 to 1818). Burns donated 177 items to the former series of volumes and 110 pieces to the latter set. The two collections bear an interesting relationship in that Thomson's work self-consciously sought to be more 'elegant' in its presentation of Scottish song than Johnston's, eschewing what were taken to be indelicate sentiments and in some cases what was taken to be disadvantageous Scots language. Johnston it was, however, who took for his aim the idea of preserving the original spirit of the items that the *Scots Musical Museum* collected and published, though a somewhat deceptive distinction in authenticity is sometimes made between the two collections since neither would conform very easily to contemporary ideas of editing and collecting songs, not least because of the huge presence of Burns in both, repairing, supplementing, improving songs he 'collected' and even sometimes fabricating their provenance. Both volumes, in fact, contribute substantially to the forging of the modern Scottish song canon, both in terms of 'art' song and 'folk' song. Debates over Burns's true intentions are perhaps also somewhat spurious, when participants divide into those who favour a rigorously traditional folk rendering of Burns's songs as opposed to those who prefer the classicized orchestral and vocal settings of Burns that emerged chiefly during the nineteenth century in the mode of high Romanticism largely taking their cue from Thomson's settings.

In fact Burns was heir in the beginning to a very heterogeneous notion of Scottish song, which he found first in a book he had pored over for years, James Oswald's *Caledonian Pocket Companion* (1759). This book blurred the boundaries between categories of 'literary' and 'folk' song, providing among other things arrangements for the 'German flute' as well as the violin. Oswald was one of the many published sources from which Burns took tunes to set words to, either his own or received material. In recent years there has been debate too over Burns's proficiency as a fiddler: was his fiddling a means to an end, allowing him to think out tunes on the one instrument in which he had rudimentary ability? Or was he passionate about the fiddle, seeing it (and traditional folk arrangements generally) as the cornerstone of renditions of his songs? No matter Burns's level of ability on his instrument, it would seem from his eclectic sourcing of music (as well as words) that, in today's terms, he was no purist, except in so far as his personal instincts were concerned. As elsewhere with Burns, the debate over genuine folk impetus and artificial enhancement has been to the fore. The fact remains, however, that there have been both excellent 'folk' and 'classical' renditions of Burns's songs over the past 200 years, and if one can see why there has been a reaction against the classical settings (since these were cued by Thomson, a man frequently snobbish in his reception of folk materials), the supplanting of one somewhat exclusive approach with another is not any more palatable, and attempts to 'tidy up' Burns all too neatly in any unitary fashion represent a distortion of a much more messy historical reality.

For the *Scots Musical Museum* in 1788, Burns produced a piece that was to become one of the most famous songs in the world, 'Auld Lang Syne' (*PS* 240). In a letter to George Thomson of September 1793, Burns claimed that he had taken 'it down from an old man's singing' (*L* ii. 246). This was precisely the kind of claim of authentic but obscure origins that made for inclusion in Johnston's volume. George Thomson, however, believed that Burns had drawn upon no such source and was adopting a playful conceit, and, as the construction of the song shows, he was probably correct. 'Auld Lang Syne' appears in the *Scots Musical Museum* with the signature 'Z', which indicated pieces to which Burns had often made substantial alterations. So, he either feels impelled to acknowledge the piece, albeit obliquely, when it goes into print, or he is perhaps enjoying leaving behind a contradictory provenance. There existed three main possible sources for the song (the second and third of which Burns certainly drew upon): a broadside ballad called 'Old Long Syne', of uncertain date; a song in Watson's 1711 volume of his *Choice Collection* which has the lines 'Should auld acquaintance be forgot / And never brought to mind?' (the same as the opening lines of Burns's version); and a love song entitled 'Auld Lang Syne' which Allan Ramsay included in his *Tea-Table Miscellany* (1724). The title of Ramsay's piece, which was a phrase of particular Jacobite and anti-Union sentiment in the late seventeenth and early eighteenth century, clearly captured Burns's imagination. Burns universalizes the sentiment so that it becomes a piece of general nostalgia, and the same goes for the depiction of drinking which he also extracts from the context of Jacobite imbibing:

> For auld lang syne, my jo,   [sweetheart
> For auld lang syne,
> We'll tak a cup o' kindness yet
> For auld lang syne.

(ll. 5–8)

Here the reference to former comradely toasts is drawn upon and supplanted by the notion of a more ubiquitous fellow-feeling (a cup of 'kindness' has replaced a cup of 'loyalty'). Burns even supplies a footnote allowing a variation: 'Some Sing, Kiss, in place of Cup', which acknowledges not so much authentic provenance as the fact that Burns seems to have remained somewhat undecided as to which alteration of his own he preferred once he had begun to veer away from the received, more narrowly ideological origins of his song. In perhaps the most celebrated of the main stanzas, Burns encapsulates the movement through life from the security of childhood to the uncertainties of adulthood with two deft strokes:

> We twa hae paidl'd in the burn,
> Frae morning sun till dine;
> But seas between us braid hae roar'd,   [broad
> Sin auld lang syne.   [since

(ll. 16–20)

'Auld Lang Syne' is a phrase eventually described by John Jamieson in his path-breaking etymological dictionary of the Scots language (1808–9) as 'To a native of this country [...] very expressive'. However, it had not been any such thing to the majority of Scots prior to thirty years earlier than Jamieson's definition when Burns widened its coinage beyond its original

Jacobite context. As so often, then, Burns is actually the inventor of tradition, here part of the 'emotional' tradition of Scotland (one might say), rather than merely its bearer.

'Auld Lang Syne' is a piece whose words are transposed from their original dedicated political nuance. More often, Burns focuses the political vocabulary of Scottish song in a way that lends it new potency. For instance, we find this in 'Such a Parcel of Rogues in a Nation' (*PS* 375), where the original Jacobite, Catholic and Episcopalian tropes of defeat by treachery and through the mercenary nature of fellow Scots is made to stand more generally as undermining not simply one kind of Scotland (Stuart-governed), but Scotland generally. An old street-rhyme can be traced to 1706, which declaims of those peers who had signed up for the treaty of Union, 'They sold the church, they sold the State and Natione, / They sold their honour name and reputatione'.[2] It is this kind of rhetoric that Burns draws on clearly in his song. However, he makes the motif of treachery not only refer to the turbulent times between 1688 and 1707, but encompass also a much longer time frame of tension between Scotland and England:

> What force or guile could not subdue,
> Thro' many warlike ages,
> Is wrought now by a coward few,
> For hireling traitors' wages.
> The English steel we could disdain,
> Secure in valor's station;
> But English gold has been our bane,
> Such a parcel of rogues in a nation!

(ll. 9–16)

Against such 'traitors' the song enjoins the memory of Robert the Bruce and William Wallace and in this widening of frame it has become a staple in the canon of nationalist song in contemporary Scotland. Overlooked today, however, is the fact that it is somewhat surprising that Burns should pen such sentiments. He had no access to any concept of practical, contemporary Scottish nationalism, or even of 'home rule', which was a development of the later nineteenth century. Burns's actual political consciousness throughout his life had to deal with a seemingly unassailable British reality, and 'Such a Parcel of Rogues' is best explained as a product of Burns's huge historical empathy with those struggling against the London government at the time of the Union and before (although, of course, here and in other places which we have already observed, Burns's icon-minting is part of the foundation of a much later *sentiment* of nationalism in Scotland). Indeed, what we probably witness in the song is obliquely registered discontent with the machinations of the British state in 1792, and the mistrust particularly of self-serving aristocrats in political power (as the Scottish commissioners of state, many of whom were non-Jacobite peers, had supposedly been at the time of the Union). The song is, perhaps, like 'Robert Bruce's March to Bannockburn', a part of Burns's response to events following the French Revolution of 1789.

Paradoxically, however, much more often in his songs Burns is explicitly Jacobite, rather than Jacobin. We see this in 'Awa Whigs Awa' (*PS* 303), which Burns composes in 1790 at a time when the Whigs in British terms are increasingly associated with the French Revolution. There is a vehement pro-Stuart bitterness in the song that explains why many long regarded Burns to be Jacobite and Tory in his politics:

> Our ancient crown's fa'n in the dust;
> Deil blin' them wi' the stoure o't,   [dust
> And write their names in his black beuk   [book
> Wha gae the whigs the power o't!

(ll. 9–12)

Burns, who was 'knighted' while touring Stirlingshire in October 1787 by the ancient Jacobite lady Catherine Bruce (who claimed descent from Robert the Bruce), seems to have been very susceptible to 'sentimental Jacobitism', and produces in their modern forms among the most famous songs in the Jacobite corpus in 'Charlie He's My Darling' (*PS* 562) and 'It Was A' for Our Rightfu' King' for the *Scots Musical Museum*. In the former piece Burns expanded a traditional street ballad that depicted the lively person of the Pretender coming to town and charming the girls. The original version is somewhat static, with a pretty woman looking out the window at the prince, who is pictured thereafter sitting her in his lap. Burns, however, inserts an intermediary stanza that confirms Charles's roguish, sexual energy in leaping up the stair of her close and 'letting himself in':

101

> Sae light's he jimped up the stair,
>   And tirled at the pin;   [lifted the latch
> And wha sae ready as herself
>   To let the laddie in.

(ll. 11–14)

Though Burns often points up the joyous energy of Jacobite song, he also augments the bitterness of the defeated cause. One place where he does this is in another song that has become a successful part of the Scottish folk repertoire, 'The Highland Widow's Lament' (*PS* 590), a piece again printed in the *Scots Musical Museum*, and almost certainly written by Burns himself. Rather like 'Poor Bodies Do Naething But M-w' in tone, this song reflects upon the devastation descending on the common Highland folk who had supported the uprising. Bitter realism collides with romantic rhetoric as a Highland woman laments the loss of her worldly possessions in the failure of the uprising and the loss of her husband:

> I was the happiest of a' the Clan,
>   Sair, sair may I repine;   [sore
> For Donald was the brawest man,
>   And Donald he was mine. –
>
> Till Charlie Stewart cam at last,
>   Sae far to set us free;
> My Donald's arm was wanted then
>   For Scotland and for me.

(ll. 17–24)

If Burns is sometimes seen as complicit in the romantic construction of Highland Scotland, he has to be seen also as someone who shows alongside the febrile sense of honour in the Jacobite cause the cost of such emotion in a balancing aftermath of deep sorrow. The stanza above is an excellent example of such telescoping effect, as 'wanted' refers both to the heroic, clarion-cry summons to battle of Donald and the absence (the 'wanting') of the woman's husband when he has gone off to fight and is killed. It also has to be pointed out that Burns's song-essays in the Jacobite mentality provoked a sympathetic response in a Lowland Scotland that had previously been uninterested in the figure of the highlander, whom it had often taken to be as racially different from the inhabitants of its locale as any 'savage' overseas. If 'Address of Beelzebub' was Burns's most passionate plea for greater consideration of the human state of the post-1745 Gaidhealtachd, it was his songs that most readily lodged themselves in Lowland consciousness and which were instrumental in the modern and historically odd development of a blanket 'tartan' identity for the whole of Scotland. It is a curious fact that Burns's own rather protean identity as a 'Scot' has been mirrored, partly as a result of his work, by Scotland itself becoming somewhat historically slippery in its identity, as it appropriates 'Highlandism' as its master signifier. If Burns, somewhat synthetically, provides for the world more than anyone else the idea of 'Lowland' Scots poetry, he does likewise with 'Highland' Scottish song.

Leaving aside 'The Heron Ballads', which Burns composed in support of Patrick Heron's election campaign of 1795 (and in which Burns, influenced by the fact that Heron had been a very accommodating host to the poet while on a tour of Galloway, lampooned those who opposed the favoured candidate of the conservatives, William Pitt and Henry Dundas), Burns's most heartfelt contemporary political song is 'Song – For A' That and A' That' (PS 482). In a letter of January 1795, Burns had written of the piece to George Thomson, 'A great critic, Aikin on songs, says, that love & wine are the exclusive themes for song-writing. – The following is on neither subject, & consequently is no Song; but will be allowed, I think, to be two or three pretty good *prose* thoughts, inverted into rhyme' (L ii. 336). Burns's 'prose thoughts' were not merely a reference to the 'prosaic' subjects outwith the spheres of 'love & wine', as Thomson no doubt thought, but, as Thomas Crawford has shown, were drawn fairly precisely from passages in Thomas Paine's *The Rights of Man* (a hidden context that would have appalled the politically conservative Thomson had he realized the fact).[3] Certainly imbued with the radical spirit of the 1790s, 'For A' That and A' That' is artfully crafted not only from contemporary political sentiment, but also from Burns's excavations of both English and Scottish song that he had undertaken for Thomson's anthologies. From the English song 'On the Seas and Far Away' (PS 454), the lament of a girl whose lover was serving his country at sea, Burns took the lines:

> Peace thy olive wand extend,
> And bid wild War his ravage end,
> Man with brother Man to meet,
> And as a brother kindly greet.

(ll. 37–40)

These hopelessly romantic, idealistic sentiments are transposed to 'For A' That and A' That' to become much more powerfully the result of common sense:

> Then let us pray that come it may,
>   As come it will for a' that,
> That Sense and Worth, o'er a' the earth
>   Shall bear the gree, and a' that.   [win first place
> For a' that and a' that,
>   It's comin yet for a' that,
> That Man to Man the warld o'er,
>   Shall brothers be for a' that.

(ll. 33–40)

Completing Burns's assemblage, the refrain 'For A' That' was taken from the Jacobite song of the same name. We see Burns, then, distilling the radical energies of the time along with emotions extracted from genres (songs of love's lament and of Jacobitism) on which he had been intensely at work for years. The melange that he produced in the song is typical of Burns's great abilities as a synthesizer of received materials to construct something extremely modern. At the same time, Burns's iconoclasm towards rank that runs throughout the song is devoid of the usual political rhetoric of the radical press of the time (it was very crafty of Burns to draw on the words of Paine, which, rather than being party political, are couched in the reasonable parlance of political philosophy). In this manner, and in drawing also on a mainstream literary didacticism (the metaphor of humans as money, below, is probably allusive to William Wycherley's *The Plain Dealer* (1674),[4] which Burns had read with interest), Burns's song seems, on the surface at least, to be without specific party impetus, even as it addresses the most pressing political matter of the 1790s, the arbitrary nature of power through hierarchy:

> Is there, for honest Poverty
>   That hings his head, and a' that;

104

The coward-slave, we pass him by,
   We dare be poor for a' that!
For a' that, and a' that,
   Our toils obscure, and a' that,
The rank is but the guinea's stamp,
   The Man's the gowd for a' that.   [gold

(ll. 1–8)

As we see in the case of 'For A' That and A' That', and as with
'Robert Bruce's March to Bannockburn' also, there are sub-
merged contexts that make Burns's song lyrics somewhat
generally 'treacherous'. Such a methodology extends even into
musical setting: for instance, the ambiguous 'The Dumfries
Volunteers', which rouses, as we have seen, a cheer for both the
king and 'the people', was set by Burns to the seventeenth-
century Royalist (and so pro-Stuart) tune 'Push about the Jorum
[punchbowl]', which adds a potentially sardonic subtext, or
perhaps counterpoint, given the song's supposedly loyal
Hanoverian surface sentiments.

Burns's formally heterogeneous impulses in song can be
found also with regard to non-political subject matter. In the
same letter in which Burns wrote to Thomson of 'For A' That
and A' That', the poet is clearly in a comprehensively
iconoclastic mood as he writes: 'I was looking over, in company
with a belle lettre friend, a Magazine Ode to Spring, when my
friend fell foul of the recurrence of the same thoughts, & offered
me a bet that it was impossible to produce an Ode to Spring on
an original plan' (L ii. 336). Taking up the challenge, Burns
produced his 'Ode to Spring' (PS 481), which begins:

When maukin bucks, at early f—ks,   [buck hares
In dewy glens are seen, Sir;
And birds, on boughs, take off their m—ss,   [mizz (slang for 'penis')
Amang the leaves sae green, Sir;
Latona's sun looks liquorish on
Dame Nature's grand impètus,
Till his p—go rise, then westward flies   [pego (slang for 'penis')
To r—ger Madame Thetis.

(ll. 1–8)

The word 'original' (meaning here 'novel', clearly) is reiterated
in Burns's letter concerning this song in which, again, and even
more directly than in the case of 'For A' That and A' That', Burns

can be seen teasing (or even taunting) the sensibilities of his prudish editor, Thomson. It has only been in comparatively recent years, and, one might speculate, in the light of the much more explicitly sexual nature of contemporary rock – rather than folk – music that 'Ode to Spring' and other songs from Burns's 'reserved' canon have been more regularly performed by artists whose repertoire extends to Burns. The song is an intriguing moment where the poet himself makes his reserved canon collide with the respectable pastoral canon with which, during his lifetime and for many years afterwards, Burns was most closely associated.

A curious fact about Burns's song *oeuvre*, observed by many commentators, is that the songwriter is at his best when not writing personally, but rather when obviously inhabiting a persona or a situation. Of the supposed exceptions to this rule are Burns's most celebrated love songs, 'Song: Ae Fond Kiss' (*PS* 337) and 'A Red Red Rose' (*PS* 453). Though 'standard' in their romantic accoutrements of situation and image, both, as Thomas Crawford has said, 'speak with the genuine voice of individual feeling [and] seem to anticipate the direct emotions of the best romantic poetry'.[5] 'Ae Fond Kiss' is produced in 1791 as Burns anticipates the departure of Agnes McLehose to be reconciled with her husband in the West Indies. The song, however, is not some spontaneous overflow of original words, but takes its cue from Robert Dodsley's 'The Parting Kiss', which contains the lines:

> One fond kiss before we part,
> Drop a Tear and bid adieu;
> Tho we sever, my fond Heart
> Till we meet shall pant for you.

Burns reworks these lines for his opening: 'Ae fond kiss, and then we sever; / Ae fareweel, and then for ever!' (ll. 1–2). Again, one is drawn to the conclusion that Sylvander's relationship with Clarinda was a highly textual affair, as Burns shows his usual craftsmanship in inventing a 'Scots' song from an 'English' model, which he cements with the tune 'Rory Dall's port', where Dall was one of the harpers or bards of Macleod of Skye, and 'port' is the Gaelic for catch, which Burns delighted in inserting, and so highlighting, as an alternative term in the *Scots Musical Museum*. What we have yet again, then, is a typically Burnsian assemblage of materials to make something 'Scots'. Burns seems not to have been so upset at losing Mrs McLehose (we should remember that he had also during the course of their meetings in Edinburgh been conducting an affair with the servant-girl Jenny Clow) that he lost his usual calm artistry. This is not to say, however, that the emotions of the song are necessarily 'insincere', but simply to point out that yet again the 'heaven-taught ploughman' notion of Burns fails. Ironically, this image in its transparent falseness has perhaps also debarred Burns from his true estimation as a proto-Romantic poet, or a poet of impeccable lyrical suffusion, as Thomas Crawford suggests. In 'Ae Fond Kiss', in fact, an intensity of feeling that comes not necessarily from his specific relationship with Agnes McLehose but perhaps from the intense emotional life that Burns had been living generally at that point is to the fore in a somewhat Petrarchan intensity:

> Had we never lov'd sae kindly,
> Had we never lov'd sae blindly!
> Never met – or never parted,
> We had ne'er been broken-hearted.

(ll. 13–16)

As James Kinsley has observed of 'A Red Red Rose', 'editors have turned up chapbook models for every stanza and almost every line of this song', and so again we see Burns taking received, this time 'folk', materials and transforming these into a larger whole.[6] We have in the song, then, one of those moments in Burns's canon where he indicates his more genuinely path-breaking 'primitive' taste, of the kind that would increasingly come to the fore in the currents of the Romantic movement. Burns wrote in November 1793 to his friend Alexander Cunningham of the song and his enthusiasm for it, that whereas 'what to me, appears the simple and the wild' would be looked on by his much more catholic tasted editor, George Thomson, as 'the ludicrous & the absurd' (L ii. 259). As a text, 'A Red Red Rose' is riotously metaphorical:

> O my Luve's like a red red rose,
> That's newly sprung in June;
> O my Luve's like the melodie
> That's sweetly played in tune.

(ll. 1–4)

To the modern eye such ecstatic language is unsurprising, but, in the light of Burns's remarks about Thomson's reception of his piece, we ought quite precisely to see Burns as part of the change in taste at the beginning of the Romantic period. Untamed emotion is registered from the first line, with the repetition of 'red', a seeming tautology of a kind that would not be found in 'literary' song anywhere else in the eighteenth century. The comparison of human emotion to vegetable and even abstract, inanimate matter (a tune) is also an exuberance (of 'pathetic fallacy') that is a marker of the new age. From the notion of harmony with nature and song, 'A Red Red Rose' moves, in a sense, to a disharmony where nature is superseded by the potency of the speaker's love, which he pledges: 'Till a' the seas gang dry, my Dear, / And the rocks melt wi' the sun' (ll. 9–10). The rather elaborate musical arrangements that have accompanied the melody (usually based on the traditional setting for the folk song 'Low Down in the Broom') tend, arguably, to 'tidy up' the jangling, somewhat overwrought emotion of the song, though more recent renditions, sparer in folk arrangement, have tended to restore its 'personal', even distracted, tenor. As with Burns's poetry, so too with this and other songs where there has been a great deal of varnished presentation, which in some crucial ways obscures rather than harmonizes with the complexities of Burns the man and his writing.

The debate over 'emotion' and 'art', and over 'roots', generally, in the work of Burns, and the formulations of all of these entities, both by the poet himself and by his interpreters (whether critics or performers), locates him as a watershed writer of the Romantic age with its new emphases upon inspiration, expressive emancipation and lyricism. Burns's juggling of an 'official' and a 'reserved' canon of work, as I have called these in the foregoing chapters, and his alternating boldness, reservation and codification in expression, reveals a set of local, national and international cultural tensions traversed by a genius. Burns's creative abilities in the context of the late eighteenth-century age of revolutionary intellectual ferment make for one of the most entangled and intriguing literary 'sites' in Scottish, British, European or world literature.

Notes

CHAPTER 1. READING BURNS

1. Edwin Muir, 'Scotland 1941', l. 30, in *The Complete Poems of Edwin Muir*, ed. Peter Butter (Aberdeen: Association for Scottish Literary Studies, 1991), 100.
2. Gerard Carruthers, 'The New Bardolatry', *Burns Chronicle* (Winter 2002), 9–15.

CHAPTER 2. BURNS THE BARD

1. Donald A. Low (ed.), *Robert Burns: The Critical Heritage* (London: Routledge, 1974), 70.
2. *The Poems and Songs of Robert Burns*, ed. James Kinsley, vol. iii (Oxford: Clarendon, 1968), 971.
3. Carol McGuirk, *Robert Burns and the Sentimental Era* (East Linton: Tuckwell, 1997), 40.
4. *Poems and Songs*, vol. iii, 978.

CHAPTER 3. RELIGION

1. Walter J. McGinty, *Robert Burns and Religion* (Aldershot: Ashgate, 2003), 228.
2. Low (ed.), *Robert Burns: The Critical Heritage*, 97.
3. See Robert Crawford, 'British Burns', in Carol McGuirk (ed.), *Critical Essays on Robert Burns* (New York: G.K. Hall, 1998), 163–81.
4. Low, *Robert Burns: The Critical Heritage*, 81.

CHAPTER 4. POLITICS

1. Marilyn Butler, 'Burns and Politics', in Robert Crawford (ed.), *Robert*

Burns and Cultural Authority (Edinburgh: Edinburgh University Press, 1997), 86.
2. See Kenneth Simpson, *The Protean Scot* (Aberdeen: Aberdeen University Press, 1988), 185–218.
3. Liam McIlvanney, *Burns the Radical* (East Linton: Tuckwell, 2002), 75.
4. Norman R. Paton, *Song o' Liberty: The Politics of Robert Burns* (Fareham: Sea-Green Ribbon, 1994), 119–20.

CHAPTER 5. WOMEN, LOVE AND THE BODY

1. *Robert Burns's Commonplace Book, 1783–1785* (Fontwell, Sussex, and London: Centaur, 1965), 16.
2. *Poems and Songs*, vol. iii, 1150.
3. David Daiches, *Robert Burns* (London: Bell, 1952), 228.
4. Thomas Crawford, *Burns: A Study of the Poems and Songs* (Edinburgh: Mercat, 1978), 146.
5. Carol McGuirk, *Robert Burns and the Sentimental Era*, 89.

CHAPTER 6. FOLK CULTURE

1. Francis Grose, *The Antiquities of Scotland*, vol. ii (London: S. Hooper, 1791), 32.
2. For a very full reading of the gender psychology of the poem, see Gerard Carruthers and Sarah M. Dunnigan, 'Two Tales of "Tam o' Shanter"', *Southfields*, 6:2 (2000), 36–43.

CHAPTER 7. SONG

1. *Robert Burns's Commonplace Book, 1783–1785* (Fontwell, Sussex, and London: Centaur, 1965), 3.
2. James Maidment (ed.), *Scottish Pasquils* (Edinburgh: William Paterson, 1868), 385.
3. Thomas Crawford, *Boswell, Burns and the French Revolution* (Edinburgh: Saltire Society, 1990), 62–3.
4. See William Wycherley, *The Plain Dealer*, ed. James L. Smith (London: Benn, 1979), Act I, Scene i: 'A lord! What, thou art one of those who esteem men only by the marks and value fortune has set upon them [...]. Your lord is a leaden shilling, which you bend every way, and debases the stamp he bears, instead of being raised by it.'
5. Thomas Crawford, *Burns: A Study of the Poems and Songs*, 269.
6. *Poems and Songs*, vol. iii, 1454.

Select Bibliography
and Discography

EDITIONS OF BURNS'S WRITINGS

Robert Burns's Commonplace Book, 1783–1785 (Fontwell, Sussex, and London: Centaur, 1965).

The Poems and Songs of Robert Burns, ed. James Kinsley, 3 vols (Oxford: Clarendon, 1968). By far, the most thoroughly annotated version of Burns's collected poems and the most cogent edition from the point of view of textual editing (though see *Robert Burns: Selected Poems*, ed. McGuirk, below). Inconsistent, however, in its presentation of the music to Burns's songs (see, in preference, *The Songs of Robert Burns*, ed. Low, below).

The Kilmarnock Poems, ed. Donald A. Low (London: Everyman, 1985). An excellently introduced and handy printing of Burns's first set of published poems.

The Letters of Robert Burns, ed. J. De Lancey Ferguson; second edition revised by G. Ross Roy, 2 vols (Oxford: Clarendon, 1985). The standard edition, highly accurate, judiciously annotated and with a series of helpful biographical sketches of the poet's correspondents.

Robert Burns: Selected Poems, ed. Carol McGuirk (London: Penguin, 1993). A selection with a very useful set of notes and which treats the chronology of some of Burns's texts differently from Kinsley, as well as selecting a different approach to textual editing which is coherent within itself.

The Songs of Robert Burns, ed. Donald A. Low (London: Routledge, 1993). An excellent first port of call for anyone seriously interested in the songs.

The Robert Burns Songbook, ed. Serge Hovey (Mel Bay: Pacific M.O., 1997 onwards). The arrangements of the late composer Serge Hovey are being completed for publication in a series of volumes under the directorship of Esther Hovey.

The Merry Muses of Caledonia, facsimile edition prepared by G. Ross Roy

(Columbia, South Carolina: University of South Carolina Press, 1999). Contains a fine pamphlet essay by G. Ross Roy; also the most handily illuminating edition of this text.

Ae Fond Kiss: The Love Letters of Robert Burns and Clarinda, ed. Donny O'Rourke (Edinburgh: Mercat, 2000). Features an excellent introduction and conveniently brings together the Sylvander–Clarinda correspondence.

Bibliography

Egerer, Joel Warren, *A Bibliography of Robert Burns* (Edinburgh: Oliver & Boyd, 1964). Now in need of updating but the most accurate guide to the publication of Burns's works in his lifetime and for the century and a half after his death.

BIOGRAPHIES

Carswell, Catherine, *The Life of Robert Burns* [1930], introduced by Thomas Crawford (Edinburgh: Canongate, 1990). This is the most readable account of Burns's life; however, in many aspects it is more like a modernist novel than a scholarly biography and it is also inaccurate in its handling of numerous episodes, not least through lashings of incautious speculation.

Ferguson, John De Lancey, *Pride and Passion: Robert Burns, 1759–1796* (New York: Oxford University Press, 1939). Although many details have been superseded by more recent work, this biography is still highly insightful in terms of Burns's poetic career.

Mackay, James, *Burns* (Edinburgh: Mainstream, 1992). The most detailed account of Burns's life yet, though sometimes proffering too much diffuse detail.

McIntyre, Ian, *Dirt and Deity: A Life of Robert Burns* (London: Harper Collins, 1995). A very readable account of Burns's life, helpful, especially, on the early life.

McQueen, Colin Hunter, *Rantin, Rovin Robin* (Irvine: Irvine Burns Club, 1999). A highly enjoyable illustrated life of Burns by an extremely fine artist.

CRITICAL STUDIES AND ESSAYS

Bentman, Raymond, *Robert Burns* (Boston: Twayne, 1987). A book that is very good on Burns's poetic form.

Brown, Mary Ellen, *Burns and Tradition* (London: Macmillan, 1984). This has sensible things to say about Burns's 'folk' context.

Crawford, Robert (ed.), *Robert Burns and Cultural Authority* (Edinburgh: Edinburgh University Press, 1997). Contains excellent essays by Marilyn Butler, Kirsteen McCue, Susan Manning and Nicholas Roe, and interesting treatments by Douglas Dunn and Seamus Heaney.

Crawford, Thomas, *Burns: A Study of the Poems and Songs* (1960; reprinted Edinburgh: Canongate Academic, 1994). The best wide-ranging survey of Burns's poems and songs; particularly excellent on ironic nuances within Burns's work, and the chapter on Burns's song-writing is superlative.

——, *Boswell, Burns and the French Revolution* (Edinburgh: Saltire Society, 1990). A very cogent treatment of Burns and the 1790s.

Daiches, David, *Robert Burns* (London: Bell, 1952). A book of great critical acumen ranging across Burns's poetry.

Jack, R. D. S., and Noble, Andrew (eds), *The Art of Robert Burns* (London: Vision, 1982). Some of the essays are now somewhat dated, but containing still some excellent criticism.

Lindsay, Maurice, *The Burns Encyclopaedia* (London: Robert Hale, 1995). Includes often excellent short essays on many aspects of Burns. The book is, however, riddled with factual errors, including numerous wrong dates, and must be used with caution.

Low, Donald A., *Burns* (Edinburgh: Scottish Academic, 1986). A highly informed and stimulating introduction to Burns.

—— (ed.), *Robert Burns: The Critical Heritage* (London: Routledge, 1974). A brilliantly chosen anthology of early Burns criticism.

McGinty, J. Walter, *Robert Burns and Religion* (Aldershot: Ashgate, 2003). The most thorough analysis of Burns's engagement with his Presbyterian background.

McGuirk, Carol, *Robert Burns and the Sentimental Era* (1985; reprinted East Linton: Tuckwell, 1997). A work that locates Burns widely in the age of sentiment and sensibility with great critical skill.

—— (ed.), *Critical Essays on Robert Burns* (New York: G. K. Hall, 1998), a wide-ranging set of essays, most of which are good, and with a very useful appendix by John Robotham, 'The Reading of Robert Burns'.

McIlvanney, Liam, *Burns the Radical* (East Linton: Tuckwell, 2002). Excellently written examination of Burns's cultural and intellectual inheritance from both his Scottish Protestant heritage and the political ferments of his day.

Paton, Norman R., *Song o' Liberty: The Politics of Robert Burns* (Fareham: Sea-Green Ribbon, 1994). No book has more detailed primary research on Burns's politics.

Simpson, Kenneth G., *Robert Burns* (Aberdeen: Association for Scottish Literary Studies, 1994). A superb little introduction, most especially on the personae of Burns's poems.

—— (ed.), *Burns Now* (Edinburgh: Canongate Academic, 1997). A diffuse but often excellent collection of essays.

113

—— (ed.), *Love and Liberty: Robert Burns, a Bicentenary Celebration* (East Linton: Tuckwell, 1997). An extremely wide-ranging collection of essays, providing the best snapshot of contemporary Burns scholarship.

Thornton, Robert D., *James Currie: The Entire Stranger and Robert Burns* (Edinburgh and London: Oliver & Boyd, 1963). A superb, highly specialized, treatment of the making of the first collected edition of Burns of 1800.

RECORDINGS

Musical renditions of Burns's work are, of course, very much a matter of taste, but the two anthologies below are particularly recommended by this commentator:

The Complete Songs of Robert Burns (Linn Records, 1995–2002). Twelve CDs of versions by a wide range of performers, all under the musical directorship of the energetically thoughtful F. W. Freeman.

Jean Redpath, *The Complete Songs of Robert Burns* (Philo Recordings, 1996). A series of six CDs by probably the greatest modern performer of Burns's songs.

Performances of Burns's songs by Isobel Buchanan, Dalriada, Dick Gaughan, Helen McArthur and Sheena Wellington are also particularly recommended.

114

Index

'Address of Beelzebub', 56–8, 103
'Address to the Deil', 15, 81–3, 84
'Address to Edinburgh', 45
'Ae Fond Kiss', 79, 106–7
Aiken, Robert, 7, 32, 40, 42
American Revolution, 55, 59
Armour, James, 8
Armour, Jean, 8, 17, 64, 66
Arnold, Matthew, 2, 55
  on 'Celtic' literature, 2
'The Auld Farmer's New-year-morning Salutation to His Auld Mare, Maggie', 15
'Auld Lang Syne', 98–101
Auld, William, 40
'The Author's Earnest Cry and Prayer, to the Right Honourable and Honourable, the Scotch Representatives of the House of Commons', 46–7
'Awa Whigs Awa', 60, 101
'A Bard's Epitaph', 22–3

Barskimming, Lord, 17
Beattie, James, 18–19, 32
  The Minstrel, 19
Blair, Hugh, 23, 35, 52, 54, 58, 82, 85
Blake, William, 31, 73
Breadalbane, John, Earl of, 56–7
Broun, Agnes, 80–1
Brown, Captain Richard, 76
Bruce, Lady Catherine, 101
Bruce, Robert, 44, 100, 101
Burke, Edmund, 67
Burnes, William, 8–9, 30–1, 32, 33, 53, 80
  A Manual of Religious Belief in Dialogue Between Father and Son, 30
Burns Clubs, 5
Burns, Gilbert, 7, 8, 30, 52
Burns, Robert
  as bard, 1, 6, 7–24, 43, 80
  'bardolatry' of, 3, 4–5
  and British national identity, 2–3, 4, 14, 18, 32–5, 55, 56, 95, 108
  and the Dumfries Volunteers, 59
  education of, 8–9, 30–1
  and Enlightenment thought, 4, 68–9
  and Robert Fergusson, 12–13
    see also Fergusson, Robert
  and folk culture, 80–94, 107
  and Freemasonry, 7, 82, 96
  as 'heaven-taught ploughman', 3, 4–5, 13, 52, 76, 80, 107
  and Highland culture, 1–2, 57–8, 71–2, 102–3
  and Jacobite song, 2, 60, 80, 100–06
  and politics, 6, 43–61, 75, 100–6
  reception of, 4–5, 6
  and religion, 1–2, 4, 12, 25–42,

44, 49, 62, 63, 65, 77–8, 81, 84–5
  and the Romantic Movement, 3, 10, 15, 19, 21, 22, 53, 54, 81, 89, 94, 97, 107, 108
  and Scots song, 43, 80, 95–108
  and Scottish national identity, 1–3, 4, 14, 18, 43, 47, 108
  and Sensibility, 3, 14, 15, 21, 28, 63, 75, 79
  use of older Scots forms, 1, 10–11, 12, 15, 36, 43, 51, 83
  and women, 62–79, 87–8, 93–4
  see also individual titles of poems and songs
Butler, Marilyn, 43
Byron, George Gordon, Lord, 19

Campbell, Margaret (Highland Mary), 8
Catholicism, 26–7, 92
Chambers, Robert and Wallace, William,
  Works, 74–5
'Charlie He's My Darling', 101–2
Christ's Kirk on the Green (anon.), 11
Clow, Jenny, 78, 106
Coleridge, Samuel Taylor, 19, 31, 34
  'Fears in Solitude', 59
'Comin Thro' the Rye', 66
Constable, Lady Winifred Maxwell, 26
'The Cotter's Saturday Night', 8, 14–15, 30–5, 36, 40, 45, 84
Covenanting Movement, 25–6, 27, 57
Crawford, Robert, 32
Crawford, Thomas, 73, 103, 106, 107
Creech, William, 24
Cunningham, Alexander, 107
Currie, James, 6, 40, 60

Daiches, David, 73
'Death and Doctor Hornbook. A True Story', 85–6
'The Death and Dying Words of Poor Mailie', 9–10, 15, 49
Dodsley, Robert
  'The Parting Kiss', 106
'A Dream', 51–2, 54
Dryden, John, 55
'The Dumfries Volunteers', 59, 105
Dunbar, William, 1
Dundas, Henry, 61, 103
Dunlop, Frances, 27, 29, 30, 43–4, 52, 55, 56, 58, 60

Edinburgh Magazine, 86
Eliot, T.S., 2
Enlightenment thought in Scotland, 4, 7, 10, 12, 14, 25–6, 27, 29, 33, 35, 38, 42, 56, 68–9, 80, 82, 84, 94
'Epistle to Davie, a Brother

Poet', 20–2
'Errock Brae', 65
'The Farewell', 96

Ferguson, Adam, 25
Fergusson, Robert, 2, 12-13, 20, 33–4, 36, 46, 84
  'The Daft Days', 49
  'The Farmer's Ingle', 33
  'Hallow Fair', 36, 83
  'Leith Races', 36
  and politics, 11, 33
  and religion, 33
Fisher, William, 40
  see also 'Holy Willie's Prayer'
'The Fornicator. A New Song', 63–4, 65, 96
'For the Author's Father', 8–9
Fox, Charles, 54, 61
'A Fragment On Glenriddel's Fox Breaking His Chain', 59–60
'A Fragment: When Guildford Good Our Pilot Stood', 54–5
French Revolution, 6, 25, 26, 44, 55, 58, 59, 67, 74, 75
Fullarton, William, 17

Gay, John, 14, 95
  'Shepherd's Week', 30
Geddes, John, 27
George III, 51–2
'Glorious Revolution' (1688), 11, 26, 100
Goldsmith, Oliver, 14, 84
  The Deserted Village, 83
Gray, Thomas, 14, 19
  'Elegy, Written in a Country Churchyard', 32
'Green Grow the Rashes', 69–70, 96
Grose, Captain Francis, 86–7
  Antiquities of Scotland, 86, 92
Guildford, Lord North, 54

'Halloween', 15, 81, 83–4, 87
Hamilton, Gavin, 40, 42
Hazlitt, William, 19
Heron, Patrick, 60–1, 103
Heron, Robert, 30
'The Highland Widow's Lament', 102
'The Holy Fair', 7, 15, 30–9, 42, 77, 83, 84, 85
'The Holy Tulzie', 39
'Holy Willie's Prayer', 3, 7, 32, 35, 40–2, 65, 84
Homer, 72
Howie, John, 27
Hume, David, 25
Hutcheson, Francis, 26
Hutton, James, 42

'It Was A' For Our Rightfu' King', 101

Jacobite Rising (1745), 2, 103
Jacobitism, 11, 80, 99–100, 100–6
  and politics, 11

115

and religion, 11
James V, 11
Jamieson, John, 99–100
Johnson, James
  The Scots Musical Museum, 3,
  44, 78–9, 97, 98, 101, 102, 106
Johnson, Samuel
  Rasselas, 54

'Kailyard' fiction, 5
Keats, John, 19
Kilpatrick, Nelly, 95
Kinsley, James, 71, 107
'The Kirk of Scotland's Garland
  A New Song', 39–40
Knox, John, 39

'Lament of Mary Queen of Scots
  on the Approach of Spring', 26
Lawrence, D.H.
  Lady Chatterley's Lover, 79
Leavis, F.R., 2
'Libel Summons', 64
Lockhart, John Gibson, 54, 58
'Love and Liberty A Cantata',
  70–3, 79, 84, 96, 97
Louis XVI of France, 59
The Lounger, 13

MacDiarmid, Hugh, 5, 58
McGinty, J. Walter, 28–9
McGuirk, Carol, 19, 76
McIlvanney, Liam, 48
Mackenzie, Henry, 13–14
  and the appellation of
    'heaven-taught ploughman',
    13–14
  The Man of Feeling, 28
M'Lehose, Agnes (Clarinda),
  76–9, 106–7
  see also Sylvander and
    Clarinda correspondence
Macpherson, James, 13–14, 57
  'Cath Loda', 16
  'Fingal', 48
Magna Carta, 56
'Man was Made to Mourn, a
  Dirge', 29
Mary, Queen of Scots, 26–7
Maxwell, William, 59
Mayne, John, 84
'Halloween', 83
The Merry Muses of Caledonia, 3,
  65–7, 69, 79, 97
Milton, John, 2, 32–3, 55, 56
  Paradise Lost, 81
Montgomerie, Alexander, 20
  'The Cherrie and the Slae', 20
Montgomery, Richard, 54, 57
Moore, Dr John, 35, 43
Muir, Edwin, 5
Muir, Robert, 44
Murdoch, John, 8–9, 31

'O Once I Lov'd', 95
'Ode for General Washington's
  Birthday', 55, 58
'Ode to the Departed Regency-
  bill 1789', 60
'Ode to Spring', 105–6
'On Seeing Miss Fontenelle in a
  Favourite Character', 74
'The Ordination', 39, 84, 85
Oswald, James

Caledonian Pocket Companion,
  97–8

Paine, Thomas, 75, 104
  The Rights of Man, 75, 103
Park, Anne, 66
Paton, Elizabeth, 17, 62, 64, 70
Paton, Norman R., 60–1
Pitt, William, 47, 61, 103
Poems, Chiefly in the Scots Dialect
  (the Kilmarnock edition), 3, 7–
  13, 29–30, 32, 35, 43, 45, 46, 47,
  51, 52, 54, 58, 67, 77, 81, 83, 96
  the Edinburgh edition, 3, 23–4,
  35, 45, 46, 52, 54, 58, 77, 82, 85,
  96
  'A Poet's Welcome to his love-
    begotten Daughter; the first
    instance that entitled him to
    the venerable appellation of
    Father', 62–3
'Poor Bodies Do Naething But
  M-w', 67, 73, 75, 102
'Poor Mailie's Elegy', 15
Pope, Alexander, 2, 14, 26, 49–50
  'Epistle to Bathurst', 50
'A Prayer, in the Prospect of
  Death', 28, 29
Presbyterianism, 25–6, 27–42,
  64, 84–5, 92
Prior, Matthew, 32

Ramsay, Allan, 2, 9, 10, 11, 12, 14,
  20, 36, 49, 95
  'Lucky Spence's Last Advice',
    9
  Tea-Table Miscellany, 99
  'The Vision', 16
'A Red, Red Rose', 106, 107–8
Reformation in Scotland, 27, 92
'Remorse', 29
'The Rights of Woman Spoken
  by Miss Fontenelle on Her
  Benefit Night', 73–4, 75
'Robert Bruce's March on
  Bannockburn', 44–5, 56, 101,
  105
Romantic Movement, 3, 10, 15,
  19, 21, 22, 53, 54, 81, 89, 94, 97,
  107, 108
Roscoe, William, 6, 60
Rousseau, Jean-Jacques, 73
- theory of the 'noble savage',
  14, 26, 80

'Scotch Drink', 45-6
Scott, Sir Walter, 5, 40
Sempill of Beltrees, Robert
  'The Life and Death of Habbie
    Simson, the Piper of
    Kilbarchan', 10, 11
Sensibility; the Age of
  Sentiment, 3, 14, 15, 21, 28, 63,
  75, 80
Shakespeare, William, 1
  Hamlet, 1
  King Lear, 15
Shelley, Percy Bysshe, 19
Shenstone, William, 2, 13, 19, 32
Sillar, David, 20
Simpson, Kenneth, 44
'The Slave's Lament', 60
Smith, Adam, 4, 29
  Theory of Moral Sentiments, 68–9

Smollett, Tobias, 33
  *The Expedition of Humphry
    Clinker*, 33
Socrates, 38
Solemn League and Covenant
  (1643), 25
'Song', 70
'Song, Composed in August', 96
'Song For A' That and A' That',
  103–5
'Song: From Thee, Eliza, I Must
  Go', 96
Spenser, Edmund, 32
Stewart, Dugald, 17
Stewart, Matthew, 17
Stewart, Thomas, 70, 79
Stuart, Prince Charles ('Bonny
  Prince Charlie'), 101–2
'Sylvander and Clarinda'
  correspondence, 76-9
Syme, John, 59

'Tam o' Shanter. A Tale', 46, 86–
  94
Thomson, George, 66, 98, 103,
  105, 107–8
  Select Collection of Scotish Airs, 3,
    97
Thomson, James, 2, 16, 19, 32,
  49, 106
  The Seasons, 19, 53
'To a Haggis', 34
'To J. S****', 16
'To a Louse, on Seeing One on a
  Lady's Bonnet at Church', 67–
  9, 79
'To a Mountain Daisy', 15
'To a Mouse, On Turning Up
  her Nest, with the Plough,
  November 1785', 15, 52–4
'To Ruin', 27–8, 29
'To W. S*****n, Ochiltree', 12
'The Twa Dogs', 39, 47–51, 52, 84
Tytler of Woodhouselee,
  William, 27

Union of Parliaments (1707), 11,
  100, 101

'The Vision', 15–19, 22, 33, 54

Wallace, William, 16, 17, 34, 43–
  4, 56, 100
Warton, Thomas
  'Ode XVII for His Majesty's
    Birthday, June 4th 1786', 51
Wars of Independence, 17, 44
Washington, George, 55–6
Watson, James, 20
  *Choice Collection of Comic and
    Serious Scots Poems*, 11, 98–9
Wilson, John, 85
Wollstonecraft, Mary
  *Vindication of the Rights of
    Woman*, 74, 75
Wordsworth, William, 19
Wycherley, William
  The Plain Dealer, 104

'Yestreen I Had a Pint o' Wine',
  66
Young, Edward,
  Night Thoughts, 28

Printed in the United Kingdom
by Lightning Source UK Ltd.
115845UKS00001B/184-222